THE LITTLE RED YELLOW BLACK BOOK

An introduction to Indigenous Australia

FOURTH EDITION

Yakarn-Moon, Jimmy Pike, Walmajarri people, circa 1981–2002. AIATSIS collection R02059-ATS 1036_332

Yakarn went travelling from west with a big mob of dogs. He started from Larripuka. He went south-east. He left all the dogs at Wanariwurtu on a hot day. He went to Nartunyju and waited for the dogs. He called them and they came up in the afternoon. He went on to Yarnantiyarnanti. He took them south now. They moved to Palpinyangu. From there he kept going right through to the Canning Stock Route somewhere.

People that side have got another story.

A tree is bent like the moon at the waterhole.

CONTENTS

Aboriginal and Torres Strait Islander peoples are advised that this publication contains the names and images of deceased people. The Australian Institute of Aboriginal and Torres Strait Islander Studies (AIATSIS) apologises for any distress this may inadvertently cause.

AIATSIS is the world's premier institution for information about the histories and cultures of Aboriginal and Torres Strait Islander peoples.

The Institute undertakes and encourages scholarly, ethical, community-based research, holds a priceless collection of films, photographs, video and audio recordings, and the world's largest collections of printed and other resource materials for Indigenous Australian Studies, as well as having its own publishing house.

Its activities affirm and raise awareness among all Australians, and people of other nations, of the richness and diversity of Australian Indigenous cultures and histories.

Australian Army Indigenous soldiers conduct a smoking ceremony at the base of the Lone Pine tree outside the Australian War Memorial, Canberra. Australian Army Indigenous personnel removed soil from the base of the Lone Pine tree at the Australian War Memorial as part of NAIDOC Week 2015 celebrations and mixed the soil at the Lone Pine site in Gallipoli, Turkey, during the Centenary of the August 1915 Offensive commemorative activities. © Commonwealth of Australia, Department of Defence

> Being welcomed to country means that it is safe for me to walk on country, that the spirits of the ancestors have provided me safe passage, and have embraced and protected me whilst I am there. It is also a mark of respect for the Traditional Owners of that country to demonstrate that I bear no ill intent and will respect their country, culture and ancestors.
>
> Jude Barlow, Ngunnawal woman and elder

WELCOME

It is important that those who are on the traditional lands of Australia's First Peoples are right-minded and cleansed. Welcome to Country rituals go back to when visitors had to wait to be welcomed into a camp or ceremony — sometimes left sitting outside the camp for days until people were ready for them and sure that they would not bring harm.

Welcomes have become strong features of contemporary Australian life and are often held at the beginning of meetings and events and may include song or dance and other local rituals such as smoking ceremonies. Welcomes can only be given by the traditional custodians of that country, or those who are given permission by the Traditional Owners to do so (see p. 20) for an explanation of the meaning of country).

Indigenous Australians acknowledge when they're on the land of Traditional Owners and, increasingly, non-Indigenous Australians do the same. These and other gestures of respect acknowledge Aboriginal and Torres Strait Islander ownership and custodianship of the land, their ancestors and traditions.

With that in mind we acknowledge the Traditional Owners of country throughout Australia and their connection to land, culture and community. We pay our respects to elders both past and present.

Alick Tipoti with his sorcerer's mask, which is made from fibreglass to replicate turtle shell. Originally from Badu Island in the Torres Strait, Mr Tipoti currently works out of Badu Island and has work in the National Gallery of Australia.
Photo: Mark McCormack

INTRODUCTION

Originally published in 1994, *The Little Red Yellow Black Book* is an introduction to the diverse histories, cultures and identities of Australia's First Peoples. The book was revised and expanded in 2008 and 2012. This fourth edition includes new and revised material.

It is impossible to produce a single narrative or to include everyone's stories. As with all communities, we do not all agree about the past, and some of us disagree strongly with what non-Indigenous commentators have said about us. The aim with this book is to provide a snapshot of some of our histories and cultures in an approachable way. The underlying themes that emerge are our adaptability and the vitality and continuity of our cultures. We believe you will find much to surprise, interest and inform you, and we hope you will enjoy reading it.

Some of us live in remote communities but many more of us live in regional towns and cities. Our hope is that Aboriginal and Torres Strait Islander readers will recognise their histories, their communities and their lives in this book, and that non-Indigenous people, whether Australian or from overseas, gain some insights into what are the world's most enduring cultural practices.

We use words such as 'coloniser', rather than 'settler', because it was the intention of the British Government to take control and ownership of this continent, which had been our home since time immemorial. Colonisation is generally viewed and described as an invasion — when an army or country uses force to enter and take control of another country. After the initial waves of colonisation and much subsequent frontier violence, the British 'settled' the country. Over the decades since then, new waves of people have arrived on our shores and become Australians.

When we talk about 'war', we don't mean trench warfare or largescale clashes between tens of thousands of soldiers; rather, we mean guerrilla tactics, where two forces of unequal power oppose each other, but not with armies on a battlefield.

Aretha Stewart-Brown taking part in the Invasion Day march in Melbourne on January 26, 2017. Photo: Darrian Traynor/Fairfax Media

This may be language you are not used to hearing when we talk about history. But it is important that we present our experience of this shared history.

We have cross-referenced parts of the book to other sections to show the links across themes, and references are included for further reading. We hope that after reading *The Little Red Yellow Black Book* you're encouraged to undertake your own research, the better to participate in, celebrate and accept our shared history and humanity.

WHO
WE
ARE

OUR PAST

When asked where we come from, our usual response is: we have always been here. Successive archaeological discoveries reveal the truth of this statement. The oldest known archaeological sites on mainland Australia date to at least 65,000 years ago — much longer than modern humans have been in many parts of Europe and the Americas. In the Torres Strait Islands, archaeologists have discovered sites that date to approximately 8,000 years, however, the settlement of this region likely extends to the earliest habitation of this continent. It is also significant that prior to global sea level rises circa. 11,000–7000 years ago, Australia (including Tasmania) and Papua New Guinea were connected, forming an even larger landmass called Sahul.

The First Peoples of Australia have adapted culturally and physically over many millennia to a range of climatic and environmental changes, including those brought about by extensive use of fire to alter the landscape. Although a level of cultural continuity and similarity across Australia is clear, regional differences demonstrate that prior to European arrival the First Peoples were innovative and adaptive to environmental and social situations. This is shown today by the sheer complexity and diversity of cultural systems, religion and distinct languages.

Aboriginal rock art, such as elaborate paintings and stone petroglyphs (carvings or inscriptions in rock), may be the first representations of this type of art anywhere in the world. It also appears that ground-stone axe technology probably began on the Australian continent earlier than elsewhere. These, along with other technologies, represent a suite of early sophisticated advances by Aboriginal peoples.

Echidna Track engraving site, Ku-ring-gai Chase National Park. Danvers Power Collection, AIATSIS, courtesy David Hardy Brown

The Echidna Track engraving site located in the Ku-ring-gai Chase National Park, NSW, has a long line of footprints which may have once linked this site to others. Sydney has been described as one of the largest open-air art galleries in the world. More than 600 rock engraving sites have been recorded in the area and new discoveries are regularly being added to the list.

Traditional Owners May Nango and her husband Mark Djandjomerr (Bolmo clan) with a stone axe found at the Madjedbebe rock shelter. Photo: Glenn Campbell/ Newspix, © News Corp Australia

A recent archaeological discovery has revealed that Aboriginal peoples have inhabited Australia for at least 65,000 years. Evidence, including stone axes and grindstones, found in the Northern Territory's Madjedbebe rock shelter, was located on the traditional lands of the Mirarr people.

WHAT WE'RE CALLED

Because our ancestors always identified themselves in local or regional terms, there was never a single name for all of us until we were labelled 'Aborigines' by the British. Aborigine is from a Latin phrase meaning 'in a place', while Indigenous means 'originating in and characterising a particular region'. It's a bit like calling people Europeans — whilst we are all Aboriginal people, we are very diverse, with different languages, cultures, spiritual beliefs and practices.

An Aboriginal person is often defined legally as a person who is a descendant of an Indigenous inhabitant of Australia, sees himself or herself as an Aboriginal person and is recognised as Aboriginal by members of the community in which he or she lives or has lived. Many visitors to this country are not aware that we have two Indigenous peoples in Australia. Torres Strait Islanders, whose cultural origins are in nearby Melanesia, come from the Torres Strait, which separates the top of Queensland from Papua New Guinea. Of the more than 100 islands in the Strait, thirty-eight are inhabited. Many Torres Strait Islanders have migrated and today live throughout mainland Australia.

> **DID YOU KNOW?**
> There have been 67 definitions of 'Aboriginality' since European settlement according to the Australian Law Reform Commission.

Government officials and people seeking a word to include both Aboriginal and Torres Strait Islander peoples use 'Indigenous Australians'. This is also the language of the United Nations in their Declaration on the Rights of Indigenous Peoples.

However, we come from many different nations and use a variety of labels to describe ourselves. Some of us identify as 'black', a word that has links with the 1970s international black rights movement, with which many of us aligned ourselves decades earlier (see p. 149).

We might call ourselves 'saltwater people' if we live on the coast, or 'freshwater', 'desert' or 'spinifex' people, if we live on that Country. As Aboriginal people from New South Wales we might call ourselves Kooris, or Koories if we are from Victoria; Queenslanders may refer to themselves as Murris, or, in the north, Bama; Tasmanians may use Palawa, and in South Australia we may use Nunga or Nyoongars in south-west Australia (also Nyungar) — note that there can be different spellings to some of these words. Some of us prefer 'Koori' or 'Murri' to 'Aboriginal' because they are names we gave ourselves and have meaning to us, as opposed to 'aboriginal' or 'indigenous' which were imposed on us and have only a very generic meaning in the English language.

But many of us would rather be identified by the nation we come from, for example a Gurindji man or a Gubbi Gubbi woman. Torres Strait Islanders prefer to use the name of their islands to identify themselves to outsiders, for example a Saibalgal (Saibai Islander) or a Meriam Le (Murray Islander). Torres Strait Islander peoples may also refer to themselves as the people of the four winds. In the 1980s Torres Strait linguist and knowledge holder Ephraim Bani coined the term 'Zenadth Kes'. Zenadth Kes, meaning the four seasons or winds, describes the region using words from different languages of the Torres Strait. Socio-political groupings are also common in the native title era — by definition these groups are bound by their laws and customs. This can be reflected in the use of the word 'nations' or 'peoples'. When referring to Indigenous Australians as a group it is acceptable to say 'Aboriginal peoples', 'Torres Strait Islanders' or 'Indigenous Australians' only if you are referring to both Aboriginal AND Torres Strait Islander peoples. If you are speaking about a specific group, you should use the correct term. When written these words are always capitalised when referring to people.

Increasingly bureaucrats and politicians are using 'Indigenous' when 'Aboriginal peoples' or 'Torres Strait Islanders' would be more appropriate, and many of us dislike this, as the word 'Indigenous' could be applied to any first peoples in the world. Many of us feel this is another way of erasing our unique identities and diversity.

Things are complicated. It's always better to ask what individuals prefer to be called, rather than making assumptions.

OUR FLAGS

We are proud of our identities as Aboriginal and Torres Strait Islander peoples and our flags are a widely recognised symbol of that. When Cathy Freeman wrapped herself in the Aboriginal and Australian flags after her 1994 Commonwealth Games win, it was an incredibly proud moment for all Aboriginal people. Most non-Indigenous Australians embraced her right to do so and did not see it as a threat to the

The Aboriginal and Torres Strait Islander flags were recognised under federal legislation in 1995.

nation, though her gesture attracted criticism. Many regional councils, schools and individuals are proud to fly both the Australian national flag and the Aboriginal and Torres Strait Islander flags, in recognition of the country's shared history and future.

The Aboriginal flag was designed by Harold Thomas, a Luritja man from central Australia, and was first flown on National Aboriginal Day in July 1971 in Adelaide. It has bands of black and red with a central yellow sun. The red at the bottom represents the earth and our relationship to it. The black above represents all Aboriginal people past, present and future. The yellow sun is, of course, the source of life. In 1997, the Federal Court of Australia officially recognised Harold Thomas as the creator of the flag. This decision meant the flag is protected under the *Copyright Act 1968* and can only be reproduced in accordance with this legislation or with the permission of Mr Thomas.

The Torres Strait Islander flag was designed by Bernard Namok from Thursday Island. It has horizontal bands, two of green for the land and one of blue for the sea. The bands are separated by black lines representing the people, and the white dari/dhoeri in the centre is a traditional headdress and represents Torres Strait Islander culture. The five-pointed white star represents the importance of navigation via the stars to the seafaring Islanders, as well as the five island groups: the northern, eastern, western, central and southern divisions. Originally made from bird feathers, dari/dhoeri are now made from a range of materials.

> **DID YOU KNOW?**
>
> The Aboriginal and Torres Strait Islander flags were legally recognised as a flag of Australia on 14 July 1995.

OUR SOCIETIES

Our worldview — the Dreaming

The Dreaming is a unique religious concept, but it goes well beyond the ordinary sense that most people understand dreams to be. Altered states of consciousness, like dreams, play a vital part in the transmission of knowledge between the spiritual and human realms.

For Aboriginal people, the Dreaming refers to a number of things. In one sense it is the creation period (a time beyond human memory) when ancestral beings spread across the continent, creating all of the plants, animals and humans, establishing societies and entrusting them with the Law — the rules for living, languages, customs and ceremonies. The ancestral beings, many having both human and animal qualities, turned a flat, featureless plain into the wonderful and varied landscape we admire today. Tired by all their endeavours, their bodies 'died', but their spiritual essence remains: in the landscape, the heavens, and the waters. We believe that their life-giving and life-sustaining powers exist at important places to this day. Our culture is based on a kind of contract: that we must follow the ancestral dictates (we use the English word 'Law' to mean this entire cultural inheritance, its injunctions and taboos) so as to stimulate and guarantee the continued flow of fertility and power from the spiritual realm. Our great founding ancestral beings are still 'out there', not interfering directly, but ever watchful. We gain our personal spirit, the life-force that animates us, ultimately from the actions of these beings. When performing our ceremonies we are calling on the creative powers to keep the land fertile, to maintain the seasons and ensure the well-being of us all. Creation stories, also referred to as Dreaming stories, differ from people to people and are

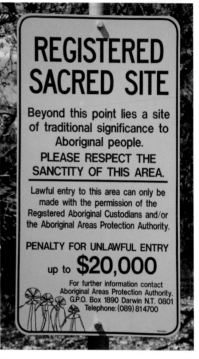

Aboriginal Areas Protection Authority Registered Sacred Site sign, Tjuwaliyn (Douglas) Hot Springs Park, Northern Territory. Photo: Michael Barritt, 2013

vital tools in teaching our children their culture and responsibilities. Art, storytelling, dance and song celebrate the central connection between the creator beings, ancestral country and us.

The Dreaming is also the 'everywhen', embracing the past, present and future. It is an enduring life-force, even though individuals come and go, and lives change. Many of us retain this essential religious outlook. As individuals and as members of social groups, we have a great many different connections to particular Dreamings, such as plants, animals and other elements of nature.

13

Bunjil by Mandy Nicholson, Wurundjeri, 1999, Koorie Heritage Trust AH2548.

The Bunjil Creation story rewritten by Aunty Joy Murphy, Senior Wurundjeri Elder

A very long, long time ago this beek [land] was like a big empty shell.

Bunjil was given a very important job to make the ngarra [mountains], the yalaks [rivers], all the creatures of the mernda [earth], a koolin [man] and a baggarrook [woman].

Bunjil couldn't do this alone. After thinking about this for a while Bunjil decided to make six tamboonamons [help(ers)]:

A tadjerri [brushtail possum]

A turnung [flying mouse-glider]

A yubup [green parakeet]

A dandan [blue mountain parrot]

A djert djert [nankeen kestrel] and

A tharra [swamp hawk].

Together they worked all yalingbu [day] and all burrun [night] for a long time. Finally Bunjil and his tamboonamons had ela monggi [created] the ngarras, the yalaks and all the creatures. Everyone was barbonneen [happy].

But Bunjil was tired, so tired he couldn't gamagoen [fly]. So Bunjil asked bellin bellin [musk crow] who was in charge of the moornmoots [winds] to help him gamagoen.

Bellin bellin opened one of his moornmoot bags.

A big gush of moornmoot blew kalks [trees] out of the beek and into the air but Bunjil's wings didn't move. Bellin bellin opened all of the bags.

A burt koreen [whirlwind] picked up Bunjil, his two wives Goonawarra and Kurook [two beautiful Swans], his son Brinbeal [Rainbow] and his wife the second rainbow, and blew them up into the tharangilkbek [heavens] to Bunjil's willam [home].

After a good ngawe [rest], Bunjil felt balit [strong] enough to ela monggi a koolin and a baggarrook.

Bunjil gamagoen down to the beek and perched on the lango [edge] of the birrarung [river of mists].

Bunjil scratched the beek and found some soft beg goreen [mud].

With his big balit [claws] Bunjil stirred all yalingbu and all burrun.

Eventually Bunjil ela monggi a round and long shape. The beg goreen shapes started shaking.

A kawang [head] and a tooleroom [body] with dharraks [arms], gurrams [legs] and djeenongs [feet] appeared. Bunjil was excited, this will be the koolin.

More shaking and slowly the koolin stood up. He yann [walked] out of the beg gorreen. Bunjil followed closely and quietly. The koolin ngormi [sat] down on the lango of the birrarung.

Bunjil was dulin [proud] and told his birri [brother] Pally yan [Bat] how he had ela monggi a koolin. But Bunjil was tired and needed to ngawe again.

Pally yan said, 'You rest my birri, I will ela monggi a baggarrook.'

Pally yan went to the same spot where Bunjil ela monggi the koolin. He found a kalkand hung upside down from a terru gulk [branch] to think about how he would ela monggi a baggarrook.

Pally yan decided to gamagoen over and around the beg goreen. The beg goreen began to shake. Squish, squish, pop, pop noises and then a tooleroom appeared. Pally yan said, 'Ah this will be a baggarrook.'

He took a piece of wooegook [stringybark] from the kalk and twisted until it was curly and placed it on the kawang of the tooleroom.

Pally yan was excited but wondered how to give murrenda [life] to this tooleroom.

He touched the upper part of the tooleroom with the tip of one of his taragos [wings]. Pally yan said, 'C'mon little one, nag ango [breathe].' Pally yan felt a doorong ting kurtini [heart beat].

The baggarrook opened her merrings [eyes], stretched out her dharraks, pushed Pally yan's taragos away and stood up.

The baggarrook looked around. She saw the koolin and yann towards him. The koolin stood up and held the baggarrook marnangs [hand]. They ngarrgee [dance(d)] until all the beg goreen had fallen from their toolerooms. They yann away leaving their djinungs koorrngees [foot prints] on the beek.

Pally yan gamagoen off to tell Bunjil the good news. Everyone was barbonneen.

Torres Strait Islanders believed in and are connected to one another by Ancestral Heroes, ancestral beings who criss-crossed the Torres Strait. Through them, Torres Strait Islanders are linked to each other and to the peoples of southern New Guinea and northern Queensland. The Ancestral Heroes gave Torres Strait Islanders laws to live by and laws that taught respect for each other, the earth and the sea. Some of the ancestors were said to be shape-shifters — at times human, at other times animal, reptile, bird or fish. This ability allowed the ancestor to dwell in, and travel through, water, earth, oil, sea and air. Like these beings, Torres Strait Islanders understand themselves to be intimately connected to the land and sea environments that are their home. These connections are everyday ones that are reinforced through fishing, gardening and turtle and dugong hunting.

Some Heroes turned into places in the sea, land or sky. Today, for example, Torres Strait Islanders look up to the warrior Tagai in the night skies. Depending on his position, they know when the seasonal rains will come and when they should plant crops. When Tagai's left hand (the Southern Cross) moves towards the sea the season's first rain, Kuki, begins.

Tagai Calendar, Robert 'Tommy' Pau, 2015. AIATSIS collection AAO R02077
ATS-1043

Traditionally, Torres Strait Islander fishermen worked out the ebb and flow of the tides by the position of Tagai, especially when sailing at night with a steady wind but little visibility. As the tide changed it would alter the boats' course. Unless the sailors watched the stars they might not notice they were going off-course. As Tagai's spear points to the South Pole, they could correct the course as the tidal direction changed.

Tagai also warns of monsoons and predicts the seasons. Crop success is dependent on the Torres Strait Islanders following Tagai's path and mapping their planting and harvesting to his movements.

DID YOU KNOW?

Aboriginal and Torres Strait Islander peoples have been described as the world's first astronomers. Dreaming stories in various locations throughout the country explain tides, eclipses, the rising and setting of the sun and moon, and planetary movements throughout the year. Research is also being conducted into whether stories can help to locate astronomical events such as comets and meteors.

Regional differences

While cultures and traditions across the country have much in common there are distinct regional differences. In the Torres Strait, many of the dances and songs refer to the local environment, including the stars when talking about the story of the warrior Tagai, while others reveal contact and influences from as far away as the South Sea Islands.

There are many Dreamings and stories for all regions. On the Larapinta Trail near Alice Springs visitors can't help but be aware of the Caterpillar Dreaming. In Arnhem Land the Yolngu record their interaction with Macassan traders with the Red Flag dance. The Titjikala community, south of Alice Springs, tell the story of the evil Itikiwarra, the knob-tailed gecko spirit ancestor, while the Anangu of northern South Australia have the Kuniya Songline, where the female python lays her eggs on a slab of rock, leaving landmarks across the country. At Gariwerd (in the Grampians) in Victoria, the traditional story of the stars of the Southern Cross is now told in both traditional dance and contemporary film.

Our contemporary art, music and dance declare that we are proud of our identity, and that our continuing connection with our lands, our islands and the seas has survived with us.

Although Dreaming stories and songs may differ, Dreaming tracks and songlines criss-cross the continent and link people and places. Dreaming

Songlines was commissioned exclusively for the sails of the Sydney Opera house as part of the Vivid Sydney Festival in 2016. Directed by Rhoda Roberts, Head of Indigenous Programming at the Sydney Opera House, this image shows artwork by Wiradjuri artist Karla Dickens. Roberts (in Vivid Sydney, 2016) said *Songlines* presented an 'unprecedented opportunity for people around the world to really connect with the culture of Australia's First People'. Photo: Daniel Boud

stories and songs may differentiate groups and places and mark out traditional territories, but there are also 'big' stories that demonstrate shared beliefs across the continent, linking people and places.

The Rainbow Serpent, for example, is spoken of across most, if not all, of Australia, often inhabiting deep dark pools in which people should not swim. The Seven Sisters story travels across the country and is shared by many peoples.

Country

Country is the term often used by Aboriginal and Torres Strait Islander peoples to describe the lands, waterways and seas to which they are connected. Country is best represented as a proper noun. The term contains complex ideas about law, place, custom, language, spiritual belief, cultural practice, material sustenance, family and identity

Country is home. It is the source of knowledge, law, science, spirituality and survival. It is integral to the transmission of cultural knowledge, skills and practices. Country is alive. It provides physical and emotional relationships with specific places and the ancestral beings that inhabit them. With the passing of the generations, deceased ancestors often become identified with the landforms, trees and spirits that animate the Country where they once lived.

Only the traditional owners can speak for and welcome visitors to Country or give others the authority to do so. They are responsible for the care and maintenance of Country. It is they who must make sure that places are looked after properly.

Tjanpi Desert Weavers Artist Camp to create *Kungkarrangkalnga-ya Parrpakanu (Seven Sisters Are Flying)*, 2015. Image by Vicki Bosisto. © Tjanpi Desert Weavers, NPY Women's Council

To look after Country means to visit it, to acknowledge the ancestors who inhabit it, to call out to the ancestors, speak their names, sing the songs, introduce strangers, welcome visitors and hold the ceremonies that keep Country healthy.

Some locations are considered dangerous and can only be approached in the company of those who know the right behaviour, if at all. Traditional owners are always concerned about and have responsibility for the safety of others on their Country.

> **DID YOU KNOW?**
>
> All Aboriginal cultural sites and relics including artifacts are protected. It is illegal to disturb or harm an Aboriginal site.

Our connections to our land

Aboriginal people traditionally lived in mobile family groups, and the ranges of movement and the size of our populations had much to do with the nature and distribution of natural resources. Groups tended to be small and widely scattered in desert areas as they needed to travel greater distances to access their resources, while communities on well-watered coasts and in the lower River Murray region were relatively sedentary in comparison, as their Country had more abundant resources. On the eastern Cape York Peninsula in the dry season people moved inland in small groups to hunt, gather and fish.

We moved around but it was always with purpose, following seasonal changes, food availability, visiting key sites to conduct ceremony, and gather for celebrations with neighbouring nations, usually at times and in places of abundance. We are both mobile while being very strongly connected, culturally and spiritually, to our Country.

All of us are connected to the land through our Dreamings. Although the forces of colonisation attempted to destroy much of that connection as the settler frontier spread through the continent, many communities continue to work hard to care for Country.

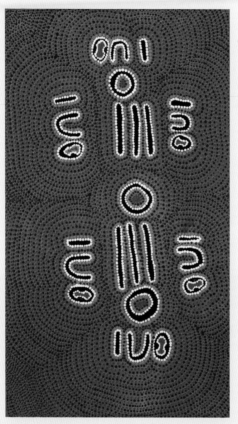

Women's Dreaming, Biddy Napanangk Timms of the Warlpiri people, 2014. AIATSIS collection R01403-ATS 691

> This Dreaming tells about a women's ceremony. Only the women know this Dreaming. It talks about travelling from north to south, east to west, teaching all the young kids. They teach people from different skin groups, so that the Dreamings are passed along to the young children.
>
> Biddy Napanangk Timms of the Warlpiri people

Seasons

The way Aboriginal and Torres Strait Islander peoples understand seasons is specific to each region and often to each group. It goes beyond the four seasons Australians are most familiar with — summer, autumn, winter and spring — or, for those in the north of Australia, the wet and the dry seasons.

The Yawuru people of Broome in Western Australia live by six seasons: Man-gala (the wet season), Marrul (changing season), Wirralburu (cooling season), Barrgana (cold season), Wirlburu (warming-up season) and Laja (hot time). The Yawuru seasonal calendar also sets out the 'right way to live' — including rules about what to eat and when, who can eat certain plants and animals, and not wasting what can't be eaten.

Spear fishing off the coast of Western Australia. Photo: James Fisher/ Tourism Australia

Lena Bloxsome (formerly) Green from the La Perouse community and Neville Bloxsome from Wreck Bay community. Photo courtesy of Stephanie Bloxsome

Family ties

Kinship is the glue that holds Aboriginal and Torres Strait Islander societies together. It locates all Aboriginal and Torres Strait Islander peoples in networks of belonging and webs of relationships that incorporate people, places, plants, animals and ancestors. Kinship systems vary from place to place, as do kin terms. It is not possible to explain all the complexities and diversities across Australia in a single book.

Most kinship systems group certain relatives together, such as same-sex siblings (women with their sisters and men with their brothers). The systems allocate roles, responsibilities and obligations to specific kin. Your uncle (your mother's brother) may have responsibility to ensure you go through certain ceremonies, for example, and generally keep an eye on you.

Kinship systems also prescribe rules about who you can marry and who to avoid. Mothers-in-law and sons-in-law may have to avoid each other in some systems. Brothers and sisters may also be in these 'taboo' or 'poison' relationships.

Some places also have 'skin' systems, which divide the world into two, with sections or subsections.

The principle of locating everyone in a universe of kin through skins – of transforming strangers into countrymen – remains, even while the relationships signalled by kin terms have become more inclusive and changed their meanings. Terms like 'uncle' and 'aunty' are extended to acknowledge and respect the seniority of elders; unrelated close friends become 'bro' or 'brother', 'sis' or 'sister'.

> **DID YOU KNOW?**
>
> In some parts of Australia the name of a deceased person may not be used. The deceased may be referred to, as is the case in parts of Central Australia, as kumanjai or 'dead person'. This practice may also extend to living people who have the same name as the deceased.

In the Torres Strait, each community is divided into a number of descent (or clan) groups that trace descent through the father's line (similar to southern Papua), with wives drawn from groups other than one's own. Each group has a name and is associated with a place and, for the Central and Western Islanders, with an ancestral totem. Rivalry was fierce between some Torres Strait Islanders, though some of it was more for show than actual fighting. Before European arrival, Torres Strait Islanders often came together to trade, for rituals (including dancing), to enhance social relationships and for enjoyment. Life changed for many with the 'Coming of the Light', when Christian missionaries arrived in 1871. They tried to put an end to some of the old ways of life, the warfare and beliefs. Today, Christianity remains strong in Torres Strait Islander communities, and a major ceremony is the Coming of the Light.

Tanika and Adrian Davis on their wedding day at the Outrigger Resort in Fiji with their son Slade Davis. Photo courtesy of Tanika and Adrian Davis

Recreating the arrival of the first missionaries on Erub (Darnley Island), this ritual is performed by Torres Strait Islanders each year when they come together to celebrate, whether on the islands or on the mainland. Despite pressure from the missionaries, many Torres Strait Islanders still actively engage in their culture and traditions.

Sorry Business, the gathering of family and friends to mourn the death of a loved one, is an important way that people express their shared cultural beliefs. As well as the actual funeral, Sorry Business often involves exchanges with and visits to show respect for particular kin. It can vary in time from days to months and even years. Sorry Business is extremely important to heal the grief of the community.

Finding family

As a result of government policies throughout the twentieth century many children were forcibly removed from their families and placed in foster homes or institutions where, too often, they suffered abuse and neglect. These children became known as the Stolen Generations (see p. 126). The devastating effect of the removal of children persists to this day and many of us continue to search for missing relatives.

The establishment of Link-Up organisations, which now operate in most states, means that expert assistance is available to those of us trying to locate missing relatives. For many, finding out about family can be both challenging and rewarding. Today, at the Australian Institute of Aboriginal and Torres Strait Islander Studies (AIATSIS), in Canberra, there is a Family History Unit, which supports Link-Up staff and the public to undertake family history research.

Many Aboriginal people undertake family history work. Ngarrindjeri Elder and researcher, Doreen Kartinyeri, made good use of the genealogies and information provided by anthropologist Norman Tindale (1900–93) about her people in South Australia, to which she added her own detailed research. Similarly, Alick Jackomos (1924–99) was a non-Aboriginal man with an Aboriginal family who conducted extensive family history research, and his work is drawn on by Victorian Aboriginal families today. He travelled widely, taking and collecting photos, hundreds of which are in the AIATSIS archives, along with the thousand intricate family trees he recorded.

Fred Leftwich's grandparents, Victor and Julie Leftwich. Photo: AIATSIS collection THOMSON.J01.BW-N04463_26

Fred Leftwich contacted the AIATSIS Family History Unit to find out more about his family. Using the AIATSIS collection, the Centre for Indigenous Family History Studies, Birth, Death and Marriage records, Trove and the Tindale Indexes, the Family History Unit was able to provide further information to Fred about his family.

Living with our neighbours

In 1606 both Dutch and Spanish vessels were voyaging within sight of the Australian coast. Sailing from Callao in Peru in 1605, Luis de Torres was second-in-command of the *San Pedrico*, which navigated its way through the sometimes dangerous reefs and islands of the Torres Strait. He sighted the hills of Cape York but took them to be a cluster of islands. The Dutch vessel *Duyfken*, commanded by Willem Jansz, was in the Torres Strait weeks before de Torres but proceeded no further than Cape Keer-weer (Cape Turn-again), on the north-west side of the Cape York Peninsula. The Dutchman Willem van Colster's exploratory voyage in 1623 is the first recorded contact with Europeans in Arnhem Land.

Daryl Guse, from the Australian National University, with the long-hidden rock art at Djulirri. Photo: Rick Stevens

A vast wall of rock art at Djulirri in the Wellington Range, Arnhem Land, includes about 1500 paintings which chronicle the history of Aboriginal contact with outsiders, from Macassan proas (outrigger boats) and European sailing ships, to 19th-century steamships and a World War II battleship.

Despite cultural and linguistic differences, the Yolngu people of east Arnhem Land traded with Macassan sailors for hundreds of years before European ships ventured to our shores. Using the monsoon winds, the Macassans sailed from Sulawesi, one of the largest islands in east Indonesia, seeking trepang (sea cucumber). In exchange, they offered the Yolngu metal knives, cloth and tobacco.

The Macassans were seasonal visitors, who came to trade but did not invade, and the clashes that occurred seem to have been an exception to a relationship that worked well, socially and economically, for both peoples. These visits are still recorded and celebrated in the music and dance of the Yolngu and other northern language groups.

Some of us joined the visitors when they went back to their own country, and marriages with the Macassans cemented the connection. We adopted the use of some words like balanda for white or lighter-skinned people (from the Macassan word for Hollander) as well as items like bamboo, clay pipes and glass. Further east, in the Torres Strait, the peoples enjoyed one of the richest marine environments in the world, with fish, crustaceans, turtles, and in some parts, dugong (sea cows). Land resources were more variable, so Torres Strait Islanders used inter-island trading networks to obtain what they lacked and to redistribute surpluses. They also exchanged valued items, like cassowary feathers, drums and ochres.

Torres Strait Islanders' ocean-going canoes allowed them to travel far afield, often in small fleets. In return for pearl shell, cone shell, turtle shell and stone, they obtained canoe hulls up to 20 metres long from Papua. To these they added double outriggers and their own distinctive form of rigging, which allowed them to become maritime explorers who could engage in long-distance trading. They navigated by the stars and used their intimate knowledge of the islands, reefs, weather, tides and currents. Also from Papua came drums, though the Torres Strait Islanders made their own special curved shark-mouth drums. The Southern Islanders traded with the Aboriginal people of Cape York to obtain spears, spear throwers

Macassans at Victoria, Port Essington, 1845, by HS Melville, published in
The Queen, 8 February 1862

and ochre, while food and decorative ornaments were traded between
the islands. Songs, dances and esoteric objects and knowledge were also
carried and exchanged along these trade routes.

After the foundation of the British colony in New South Wales, the
Torres Strait became a common, if dangerous, route for ships, because
of the reefs as well as raiding parties led by Torres Strait warriors.

By the 1800s, some of the visitors married Torres Strait Island
women, however most marriages were with other Pacific Islanders,
including Rotumans, Samoans, new Hebrideans (from Vanuatu) and
Lifuans (from Noumea).

Living off the land and sea

The British claimed mainland Australia as their own, considering it to
be *terra nullius* (land belonging to no one), ignoring our systems of
land ownership and our intimate attachment to Country across the

entire continent. Today, you can still see some of the old stone tunnels, channels and ponds we used to modify waterways in various locations across the country, and stone fish traps around Mer, Erub and Ugar Islands in the Torres Strait. The Gunditjmara people of western Victoria conduct tours of the water-races (canals) made by their forebears and the stone dwellings they lived in during the fishing season.

Fish traps on Erub (Darnley) Island in the Torres Strait. Photo: Polly Hemming

When anthropologist Alfred Haddon visited the Torres Strait, he noted that stone fish traps lined the shores of 'practically every island'. During high tide the walls of the fish traps are completely submerged. As the tide falls, exposing the walls, the fish are confined within the traps. As the tide drops even further the fish can be easily captured by net or spear, or occasionally poison.

Recently the people on Erub have had to compete with feral dogs on the island stealing fish from the traps. Introduced species such as cats, dogs, pigs, rats and deer have had a tremendous impact on the island ecosystems of the Torres Strait.

We used the resources of both the land and sea. Some of us travelled widely, using our extensive knowledge of the seasons and weather to work out when the best time was to move to a different location. All groups knew the movements of others and larger groups gathered for ceremonies or to feast on particular foods that were plentiful at certain times of year.

We are experts in the use of fire to manage our country, using low-intensity fires to clear the undergrowth, promoting the regrowth of some plants and encouraging the grazing on open pastures (and thus the easier spearing) of game animals. Kangaroos, particularly, like to eat the new growth of grass. The English surveyor William Sharland observed these practices by Aboriginal people in Tasmania. In one diary, he noted:

The valley had all the appearance, at a distance, of undergoing all the various processes of agriculture — some parts (the most recent burnt) looking like freshly ploughed fields; and again, other parts possessing the most beautiful verdure from the sprouting of the young grasses and rushes (Sharland in Gammage 2011)

These practices required intimate knowledge of how local plants and grasses reacted to fire as well as highly developed scientific skills to observe and adapt practices in changing environments. The outcome of these practices over a millennia has seen an increase in species that recover quickly from fire such as certain yam and seed-producing plants.

This practice of utilising fire to manage the environment continues today. Firestick farming, as it is now called, is a purposeful strategy for increasing the availability of edible food and is an essential feature of caring for Country. Today, Aboriginal and Torres Strait Islander ranger groups frequently utilise fire to manage invasive species, promote native plants and wildlife that require fire, and mitigate large scale destructive fire events.

Because many Aboriginal people were frequently on the move, our toolkits were lightweight and multipurpose. Hunters used carved

Nolia Napangati Ward burning. Photo: Dr Rachel Paltridge

Kiwirrkurra Traditional Owners continue to conduct extensive patch-burning on the Kiwirrkurra Indigenous Protected Areas (IPA), both during ranger work and through their daily hunting activities to harvest goannas, blue-tongued lizards and feral cats. Firescar mapping has revealed that 516 fires occurred within a 20km radius of Kiwirrkurra from 2010 to 2015, and that the median fire size was only 4.6 hectares. By comparison, in the same sized area of remote, unmanaged country to the north, 13 lightning-induced wildfires occurred during the same five-year period, and the average fire size was over 8,000 hectares. The burning promotes growth of a key food plant for the bilby, which has continued to persist at numerous sites within the Kiwirrkurra hunting zone.

South Coast Aboriginal fishers with a haul of mullet at Mullimburra Point, NSW.
Photo courtesy Wally Stewart, 2013

wooden hunting tools like spears, clubs and boomerangs. Women carried digging sticks and wooden containers or baskets. In some areas their spinning and weaving produced twine, nets and bags for carrying food. Nowadays, some women prefer using iron digging sticks and men favour guns, which makes it easier to hunt large introduced animals like buffalo, cattle, camels and pigs that run wild, causing a lot of damage to the native animals and environment.

Many of us still catch or gather traditional foods today: turtle, dugong, shellfish, magpie geese, grain, fruits, tubers, file snakes, oysters, mussels, duck, kangaroo, echidna, murnong (yam daisy), eels, salmon, whiting, abalone, mullet, shark and much more. Some foods, like dugong and turtle, are found only in the north, while others, like abalone and eels, are more common in the south of the country.

The Scottish-born explorer John Mckinlay (1819–72) saw people herd baby pelicans into a brush yard, keep them and use the young birds for food just before they could fly. Other explorers recorded seeing people pulping figs into a long-lasting preserved cake. Meat was dried, smoked and salted. We dug yams and promoted the growth of other tubers where we found them. We have vast stores of knowledge about how to live on this continent, and part of this is revealed in the diaries of the non-Indigenous explorers, which in some cases offer detailed descriptions of hunting and gathering activities, like firestick farming.

> We've been doing it in this country thousands of years more than white men put together have been doing it. We know how fish react, we know how they travel, we know where they travel, we know what time of year they travel. Twice the European people tried to settle at Broulee and they would have starved only for the Aboriginal fishermen. We go back a long way.

Tom Butler, Budawang-Murramarang Elder

Aboriginal and Torres Strait Islander peoples have lived off their waters for millennia. We developed an intimate knowledge of the species we fished, and skills and techniques were passed down and perfected over thousands of generations. On the NSW South Coast, Aboriginal fishers used their cultural knowledge to start the commercial fishing industry, and they passed the trade down to their children. Tom Butler, a Budawang-Murramarang Elder and retired commercial fisherman, is one of their descendants.

Cultural and natural resource management today

In many parts of Australia, Aboriginal and Torres Strait Islander people continue to be heavily involved in the management of their traditional lands and waters. These opportunities have been created largely due to the acquisition of land and water through legal systems such as native title and land rights. Co-managed national and state parks have also provided opportunities for Aboriginal and Torres Strait Islander peoples to manage their Country. Some of the largest cultural and natural resource management programs include the national Working on Country, Caring for Our Country and Indigenous Protected Areas programs, as well as various state/territory land and water management initiatives.

Many of these cultural and natural resource management groups, commonly known as ranger groups, are administered and supported through land councils. Where they are not supported by land councils, they can be supported through co-managed national parks, local Aboriginal and Torres Strait Islander corporations, native title corporations, regional authorities, or are established as their own independent organisation.

Bush tucker

Aboriginal people visit and care for specific localities to take advantage of seasonal foods. When these foods — cycad palms in the north, bogong moths in the Alps, grain harvests of the inland, eel trapping in the south, crayfish and shellfish collections on the coast, just to name a few — were at their most plentiful, it was an occasion to invite neighbours to share the bounty. These gatherings were announced by messengers who were given the right to travel safely through the lands of others. These gatherings allowed us to trade, acquire and exchange new songs, dances, valued artefacts and other forms of culture, to meet relatives and to arrange marriages.

All members of our communities had particular responsibilities for collecting and preparing food, and the division of labour was largely gender-based: men usually hunted large game while women hunted small game and gathered food. Depending on the area and the season, we had access to highly nutritious food.

Freshly picked cheese fruit in Kowanyama, North Queensland. Photo: Andrew Bibington/AIATSIS

The Torres Strait Islands vary in their geography and their capacity to sustain people, some of them having little water and poor soil. There was a strong trade in food and other items between islands, and with people further afield, that some Torres Strait Islanders continue to this day.

The Eastern Islanders were able to grow yams, bananas and other crops, while on the Western Islands there were wild yams and other edible roots, as well as mangrove pods. Throughout the islands our protein came from the sea: in particular, molluscs, fish, turtle, dugong and so on.

Chef Mark Olive. Photo: Mark Olive, 2017

Bundjalung chef Mark Olive has been working with native ingredients in Australia for decades. Olive believes that it is time for Australia to embrace bush foods:

> We've embraced every other culture in our country. We've got Asian, we've got curry in our cupboards, but nobody's got wattle seed. I think it's time we jumped on board. ...[L]ooking at our foods, [you] can see the different tones, textures and aromatic scents...It's the curiosity factor for everybody right now, but not only that, it tastes great!

Contact

The fencing-off of land by colonists restricted Aboriginal people's access to fresh water and food. When the colonists let their animals out to graze on the land or drained swamps to make more pasture, waterways were affected and many staple vegetable foods disappeared, reducing the variety in our diet and increasing the risk of deficiencies and disease. For example, sheep cropped the basal leaves of the murnong (yam daisy) so closely that it disappeared completely from most districts of south-eastern Australia.

DID YOU KNOW?

In 1984 a group of Pintupi people from the Western Desert made contact with settler society for the first time. The family had been living in the Gibson Desert region and became known in both national and international media as the Pintupi Nine after they connected with their kin who were living in the Kiwirrkurra Community in Western Australia.

Land was cleared of trees and scrub that were key environments for many animals. With their destruction, we lost access to some of the basic components of our diet, and came to rely on the colonisers' less nutritious white flour, tea and sugar. The impact of the disappearance of and restricted access to food cannot be underestimated.

By the 1820s and 1830s, some Torres Strait Island communities were in contact with passing European ships. They traded fresh food and other items for iron. Trepangers, those seeking bêche-de-mer or sea cucumber (considered an aphrodisiac by Chinese people), were working for long periods in the Torres Strait from the 1860s, sometimes in great numbers. They were equipped with guns, and the Torres Strait Islanders were at a disadvantage compared to these better-armed invaders. Between the London Missionary Society and the government, the Torres Strait was transformed during the last quarter of the nineteenth century; however, many Torres Strait Islanders were able to stay on their traditional island.

INDIGENOUS AUSTRALIAN LANGUAGES

At least 250 languages, many with numerous dialects, were in use on the continent and islands prior to European colonisation. Indigenous Australian cultures are multilingual, speaking the languages of neighbours is a cultural norm; in some areas, like Arnhem Land, many different languages are spoken over a small area, whereas at the other extreme is the Western Desert Language whose many dialects (such as Pitjantjatjara) are spoken across about one sixth of the continent, covering much of the desert regions of Western Australia, South Australia and the Northern Territory.

There are two languages in the Torres Strait: Kala Lagaw Ya is related to Aboriginal languages and spoken on the western islands of Mabuiag and Badu; Meriam Mir is related to the Papuan languages and is spoken throughout the eastern islands of Erub (Darnley), Ugar (Stephen) and Me In a small number of remote communities, the traditional language is maintained as the first language acquired by the youngest generation. In other communities there are only a few Elders who still speak the traditional language, but younger generations are working to learn it. In some communities the traditional language is no longer spoken, but revivals are underway based on the memories of

DID YOU KNOW?

At the time of European arrival in Tasmania there were eight distinct language groups on the island. Today Palawa Kani, run by the Tasmanian Aboriginal Corporation, is a project to reconstruct a language based on what is known of Tasmanian languages.

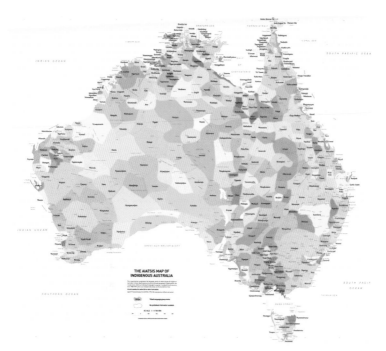

The AIATSIS map of Indigenous Australia. This map attempts to represent the language, social or nation groups of Aboriginal Australia. It shows only the general locations of larger groupings of people which may include clans, dialects or individual languages in a group. It used published resources from 1988–1994 and is not intended to be exact, nor the boundaries fixed. It is not suitable for native title or other land claims. David R Horton (creator), © AIATSIS, 1996

Elders and historical records, which are compared with known attributes of spoken and well documented languages.

Austlang is a database of Indigenous Australian languages and contains the most comprehensive range of information, datasets and references for over 1200 language varieties. Austlang functions as a pathway into MURA, the AIATSIS catalogue and as a source of information for each language variety, including location (supported by a digital map), relationships with other languages, and a history of documentation.

Australian Army soldier Gunner Marc Jones and his grandfather Major Don Cruden (retired) at Kapooka, near Wagga Wagga, NSW, on 30 June 2017 at the NAIDOC Week celebrations.

The 2017 NAIDOC theme 'Our Languages Matter' reflects the importance of language to Indigenous Australian communities. Our languages are not just a means of communication, they express knowledge about everything: Law, geography, history, family and human relationships, philosophy, religion, anatomy, childcare, health, caring for Country, astronomy, biology, zoology, cuisine, construction, design, just to name a few. Support from the wider community in the form of government policies, methodologies in education (especially vernacular literacy development) and the creation of domains for the expression and inclusion of Indigenous languages will support maintenance, revival and reconstruction efforts. The link between cultural expression and well-being is evident across Australia, and more Australians from the wider community are interested in learning about Indigenous Australian cultures and languages and the land we share.

In 2012 Federal Parliament's House of Representatives Standing Committee on Aboriginal and Torres Strait Islander Affairs called for the protection of endangered Indigenous languages, and recommending bilingual education. In 2013 the Australian Curriculum, Assessment and Reporting Authority (ACARA) included 'Aboriginal and Torres Strait Islander histories and cultures' as one of the three cross-curriculum priorities in the Australian Curriculum. In 2015, the Framework for Aboriginal Languages and Torres Strait Islander Languages was added to the Australian Curriculum to guide the learning and teaching of local Aboriginal and Torres Strait Islander languages across Australia. The teaching of Indigenous Australian languages can now be seen in primary, secondary and higher education in many schools.

> **DID YOU KNOW?**
> Many Indigenous Australian groups have sign languages. In addition to this, most groups have sets of signs that they use alongside their spoken language. These signs may include pointing with the lips, turning the hand palm down to indicate a negative, or turning the index finger to point upwards to indicate a question as well as signs to indicate particular relatives or animals.

Aboriginal English

In modern times many Indigenous Australian people include a variety of Aboriginal English in their language repertoire alongside a traditional language, Kriol and/or Standard Australian English.

Aboriginal English affects the semantic range of some English words, such as 'grannies' and 'deadly' which have very different meanings in Aboriginal English. 'Grannies' for example means grandchildren, not

Tjinari (meaning 'someone always on the go' in the Ngaanyatjarra language) is a language game app. In each level a 'runner' faces culturally relevant obstacles that must be resolved in order to find a special plant medicine to give to a traditional healer to save a young girl. The origin of the *GameMaker: Ngarlpuputju* project was a 2015 collaboration between an ARC-DI 'Western Desert Speech styles and Verbal Arts' project and students from the ANU College of Engineering and Computer Science and School of Art. Photo: Conor Tow, ANU art student

grandmothers, while the word 'deadly' means something that is positive. Aboriginal English incorporates sounds, words, word and sentence building strategies from local traditional languages, alongside distinct communication styles, which accounts for variation across Australia. The term 'Aboriginal English' represents a continuum from some varieties close to the various creoles, to those which resemble Standard Australian English in many aspects.

Diana Eades is a forensic linguist whose book, *Aboriginal ways of using English*, addresses the way Aboriginal speakers use and speak English. A key point Diana makes is around the use of silence. In Western societies, silence is an uncomfortable thing that people rush to fill, but in most Indigenous Australian cultures, silence is a key part of conversations, and to rush to fill it is considered rude.

The majority of Aboriginal people in Australia speak a variety of Aboriginal English as their first language, however, in more remote areas it may be a second, third or fourth language for those who speak one or more languages and/or a creole.

Kriol and Torres Strait Creole

Creoles develop from simple contact communication systems (called pidgins) used between people who do not have a language in common. In northern Australia the contact pidgins developed from English and Indigenous Australian languages. There are creoles which are national languages, for example Bislama in Vanuatu, Tok Pisin in Papua New Guinea, Krio in Sierra Leone and Afrikaans in South Africa, which is also described as a creole.

Two girls at the launch of *Tudei en longtaim* and *Yakai! Beibegel!* — Kriol language books written by a group of women from Binjari community. Photo: Indigenous Literary Foundation

One early contact pidgin expanded into a creole at Ngukurr (Roper River Mission) in the early twentieth century. Aboriginal people were being brutally driven from their own country by the pastoral industry and many put their children into the Roper River Mission for safety. Here children from many different nations were thrown together, with their only form of shared communication being a pidgin. Pidgins are very limited forms of communication so the children expanded the pidgin's grammatical and lexical ranges to form a fully functional language to suit all communication needs. Languages which develop in this way are called creoles. Linguists have shown that creoles are fully functional, rule-governed languages, with complex grammars, but for social reasons they are not held in high esteem, often being described as 'bad English'. This is problematic when we consider that in northern Australia this creole, now known as Kriol, is the first language for many thousands of people.

Samuel Brazel, Anaiwan, Management/Indigenous Consultant; Tyrone Bean, Kabi-Kabi/Bindal, Secondary School Teacher; and Liam Coe, Wiradjuri, Architecture Student. Photo courtesy of Samuel Brazel

Torres Strait Creole is a widely spoken language in Queensland, used by over thirty thousand people as a first, second or third language alongside Standard Australian English, Kala Lagaw Ya and Meriam Mir, although it has less status than these traditional languages. It is a direct descendant of Pacific Pidgin English, the lingua franca of the Pacific from the turn of the nineteenth century when it arrived in the Torres Strait. It became the first language of a generation of children and thus expanded its functions beyond a contact language (pidgin) and became Torres Strait Creole. Due to its provenance it is related to Tok Pisin in Papua New Guinea, Bislama in Vanuatu and Solomon Islands Pijin. This language is also known by the name YumplaTok.

Place names

Words and phrases from Indigenous Australian languages have been incorporated into placenames since European colonisation and changed to suit the range of sounds in English and their expression in written form. This process has enriched Australian English providing it with unique words not found elsewhere. Take for example the word Toowoomba, a large town in south-east Queensland. Its name originally comes from the English word 'swamp' (the nature of the country) which was translated into the local Aboriginal language to become something like 'toowampa'. This was then borrowed back into English as Toowoomba. Different languages have different sets of sounds and different rules for how they may be arranged. So, when a word is borrowed from one language (in this case English) to another, it changes to suit the sound system of the borrowing language. In this instance the local language does not have the sound 's' so this is replaced by 't'. The local language also requires a vowel between the 's' and 'w' (oo) and at the end of the word (a). The result of these adaptations is a form like 'toowampa'.

s		w	a	m	p	
t	oo	w	oo	m	b	a

From Dubbo — taken from a Wiradjuri word 'thubbo' meaning head covering, to Canberra — a Ngunnawal word meaning 'meeting place', to Wollongong, — derived from the Wodi Wodi word woolyungah, meaning 'five islands' — these names evoke our heritage.

In recent times dual naming has been adopted to include a local Indigenous name alongside the English name in many parts of Australia. For example, Ayers Rock is more often referred to by its historical Anangu name in Pitjantjatjara language, Uluru. In New South Wales, a bridge called Macleay River Bridge includes a description in Dhanggati: yapang gurrarrbang gayandugayigu or very long track to the other side, which refers to the structure being the longest bridge on the continent.

Kevin Yow Yeh, Wakka Wakka man, volunteered in an Indigenous South African primary school in Mpumalanga in 2016. Photo courtesy of Kevin Yow Yeh

HOW
WE
LIVE

POPULATION

While it can never be known for certain, some researchers estimate that the Aboriginal and Torres Strait Islander population at the time of colonisation was 500,000 people. By 1933, after colonial violence, dispossession from our lands and with the effect of introduced diseases, experts estimate that our population was at its lowest point, at only 20 per cent of what it was in 1788. Before the 1967 Referendum we were not counted as people, but listed as 'flora and fauna'. We were first counted as a discrete population in the national 1971 Census, and since then an increasing number of people have identified as Aboriginal and/ or Torres Strait Islander. There was an 11 per cent increase between the 2001 and 2006 censuses, a 20.5 per cent increase between 2006 and 2011, and an 18.4 per cent increase between 2011 and 2016. This cannot be accounted for by an increase in birth rate alone. The Australian Bureau of Statistics (ABS) attributes the increases to the growing number of people who are self-identifying as Indigenous Australians, and to greater efforts being made to record Indigeneity in the censuses. Identification as an Indigenous Australian is voluntary, and the ABS

Stephanie Bloxsome, Jemma Milloy, Barbie-lee Kirby and Kevin Yow Yeh at the annual Koori Knockout in 2016. Photo courtesy of Stephanie Bloxsome

calculates 'experimental estimates' for the size of Aboriginal and Torres Strait Islander populations. The 2016 Census counted 649,200 Aboriginal and Torres Strait Islander peoples, representing 2.8 per cent of the population. Their experimental estimates and projections are that the Indigenous Australian population will increase at an average annual growth rate of 2.2 per cent to the year 2021, compared to 4 per cent of the total Australian population. Because some of our population are mobile, it can be difficult to obtain accurate data, but inaccurate data collection leads to significant outcomes such as inadequate provision of services of housing and health.

Generally, we have a much younger population age structure than non-Indigenous Australians, with a median age of 23 years compared to 38 for the rest of Australia. This is attributed to high levels of fertility and mortality.

> **DID YOU KNOW?**
> Sixty per cent of Aboriginal and Torres Strait Islander people use Facebook on a daily basis, compared to the national average of forty-two per cent. Across remote communities, where computer ownership is low and internet may not be available, forty-four per cent of Aboriginal and Torres Strait Islander people use Facebook.

REMOTE, REGIONAL AND CITY LIVING

Throughout the two-plus centuries since colonisation, but particularly in the past few decades and in the south-east of the country, we have moved from remote and rural areas to large country towns and to more urban and metropolitan centres. Originally, this reflected forced removals and dispossession from our lands. More recently, both Aboriginal and Torres Strait Islander people have moved in search of employment and better education.

Senior Gupauyngu man Eddie William Gumbula performs the Sugarman Dreaming story during the closing bunggul of the 2018 Garma Festival in north-east Arnhem Land. Photo: Melanie Faith Dove/Yothu Yindi Foundation

We make up most of the population in Australia's remote areas, from the Torres Strait down to Tasmania and through to the desert regions of Western Australia, and a significant population in other remote areas. Over the decades, some regional areas were cleared for agriculture, destroying food sources and sacred sites. It's estimated that 30 per cent of our population lives in regional areas. In the areas where the missions and reserves were set up, there are more of us. Although just over half of our total population lives in two states, New South Wales and Queensland, we make up only a small proportion of the overall populations of these states. Whereas only 9 per cent of us live in the Northern Territory, we make up more than a quarter (26 per cent) of the total population. In all other states and territories we're less than 5 per cent of the population.

The majority of Torres Strait Islanders now live on the Australian mainland, mostly in urban centres along the coast of Queensland and New South Wales, with Cairns and Townsville having lively Torres Strait Islander communities.

Recognising urban Indigenous Australian identity

Defining Indigenous Australian people by location, descent or appearance does not reflect the complexity of Aboriginal or Torres Strait Islander experience and identity. Identifying people as Indigenous Australian by the way they look is an out-dated concept because it doesn't acknowledge who people really are. Despite it being a flawed exercise in stereotyping, some public figures and commentators continue to show little or no understanding of Indigenous Australian identity and needs, particularly in urban settings.

Zac Collins-Widders, Anaiwan person, graduating from the University of Melbourne with a Bachelor of Arts. Photo courtesy of Zac Collins-Widders

Neville Bloxsome with his grandson, Chris Bloxsome and great grandson Narli Deaves enjoying the day at the Nowra Pool in 2016. Photo courtesy of Chris Bloxsome.

Many economic and social issues influence our Aboriginal and Torres Strait Islander identities. Like Indigenous people elsewhere, urban-living people face racism, isolation, marginalisation and failure to connect with the community. However, despite these challenges, Aboriginal and Torres Strait Islander pride, identity and culture have survived and thrived in urban environments.

Urban Indigenous identity is an issue for people in other countries, too, not just Australia, for example, in Canada, New Zealand and the Americas. It is a challenge that the Sami and Inuit of the Arctic are also facing and meeting.

Back to Country

In 1976 the Australian government passed the *Aboriginal Land Rights (Northern Territory) Act 1976*. In a move back to Country, in the 1970s many people left the northern towns and mission settlements and established outstations on ancestral lands. Here we could maintain our culture without the distractions and conflicts of modern town life. Today, over 12,000 people live on more than 1,000 outstations.

The Kuninjku people of western Arnhem Land have several outstations that have become increasingly prosperous. They sell artworks, work in tourism and environmental management projects, as well as harvesting food in the traditional way. The outstations have had a positive effect on Country as a result of traditional land care, while the transfer of cultural knowledge from old to young helps sustain Kuninjku culture.

In March 2008, the *Medical Journal of Australia* reported that the Alyawarr and Anmatyerr people on the sixteen outstations of Utopia,

Personnel from the RAAF and Worimi community perform in the Fish Dance, an integrated RAAF/Worimi indigenous dance, put on as part of NAIDOC Week celebrations at RAAF Base Williamtown, NSW. Photo: Australian Government Department of Defence

290 kilometres north-east of Alice Springs, had a mortality rate almost half that of other Northern Territory Aboriginal peoples. The report explains why they are living longer: they exercise more, eat a considerable amount of traditional food and have medical services that actively work to prevent disease.

While many of us live urban lives and are employed alongside other Australians, some groups have been able to continue traditional or semi-traditional lifestyles. Yet we are no less Aboriginal or Torres Strait Islander if we live in towns or cities. Many who are city dwellers are still living on Country, regardless of how it has been transformed. Those of us who come from other areas return to our communities for times of ceremony and family business. We have successful doctors, lawyers, politicians, businesspeople, teachers, scientists, artists, environmentalists and sportspeople. Wherever we live we retain connections to our Country, sustained by our culture, our kin and the spirit of our ancestors.

Douglas Briggs at the Eiffel Tower in Paris, France. Photo courtesy of Douglas Briggs

HOUSING

The majority of Aboriginal and Torres Strait Islander people live in major cities and regional areas (see Population, p.52). Places of residence include settlements (now referred to as 'communities'), like old missions, government reserves and town camps, and urban housing scattered across suburbs in regional towns and cities. Today most of us, especially those of us that live in urban areas, reside in western housing. In a lot of regional and rural communities housing can be an issue, as it is often provided by the government and not maintained as it should be.

In many ways our traditional forms of shelter were much better suited to the landscape and climate than colonial architecture, which was based on designs for the northern hemisphere's colder climate.

Traditional island dwellings in the Torres Strait were strong, with either a bamboo or mangrove framework and poles, and thatched roofs and walls made of palm leaves and grass. Structures were unique to particular areas, for example, those in the north were built on poles above the ground, whilst those in the east were shaped like beehives.

In north-west Tasmania people scooped out the soil so they and their fires could be below ground level, and people built strong beehive dwellings above, plastered with mud. Some could fit a family, others

'Encampment', William Wyatt, 1862. Photo: National Library of Australia, 8632 #R11313

59

Newly constructed house of plaited coconut leaves in traditional style, belonging to Wilfred Tapau and his family on Mer (Murray Island), Torres Strait, Qld. Photo: AIATSIS collection SHNUKAL.A03.CS-000069292

Remains of an Aboriginal stone house in the Budj Bim Cultural Landscape, Victoria. Photo: Damien Bell, 2015

allowed for people to get together en masse. At Lake Condah and nearby in western Victoria, people built seasonally inhabited villages of stone dwellings with timber roofs.

Diaries and official colonial records report the existence of more substantial and permanent housing in western Victoria, but over most of the continent, our mobile adaptation meant that it was not worth the investment in time and energy to build permanent dwellings.

HEALTH

Overall, we are less healthy than other Australians, though there have been small improvements in recent years. Our continuing poor health cannot be understood solely in medical terms. There are also other issues such as education, employment, income and socioeconomic status that affect our health and well-being, for example our history of dispossession, colonisation, failed attempts at assimilation, racism and the denial of citizenship rights.

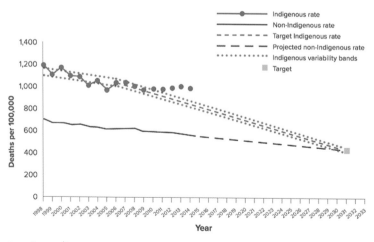

Overall mortality rates by Indigenous states: NSW, Qld, WA, SA and the NT combined 1998–2021. Source: ABS and Australian Institute of Health and Welfare (AIHW) analysis of National Mortality Database

Jamahl Ross, Aboriginal and Torres Strait Islander Health Worker, based at
TAIHS (Townsville Aboriginal and Islander Health Service) in Townsville, Qld.
Photo: Townsville Aboriginal and Islander Health Service

Data from the Australian Bureau of Statistics (ABS) (2016) estimates that the median age at death for Aboriginal and Torres Strait Islander males was 54.9 years in 2013–2015, an increase from 50.9 years in 2003–2005; there was also an increase for females to 61.5 years from 58.4 years over the same period. The non-Indigenous median age at death was substantially higher at 81.9 years in 2013–2015. Our infant mortality rate is 1.9 times that of non-Indigenous babies and we have a higher percentage of low birth-weight babies compared to other Australians. However, recent years have seen these mortality rates more than halved. Diseases of the circulatory system are the main causes of death, with diabetes, influenza, pneumonia, asthma, bronchitis, emphysema and suicide next. In 2016 the ABS acknowledged that non- and late registration of Indigenous deaths has affected the reliability of its data over time.

While there have been recent improvements in the lives of those of us living in parts of the country, the figures for other Australians have also improved, so the gap has not narrowed significantly. By comparison, the Indigenous peoples of New Zealand, Canada and the USA, countries with similar colonial histories to Australia, have smaller differences in life expectancy and infant mortality.

For Australia to move forward as a caring society, the gap between our health and that of other Australians needs to be closed. This will require working together on both the medical and social issues that impact on our health, and long-term funding is required in a wide range of preventive and clinical services.

The 'Closing the gap' commitments by the Council of Australian Governments (CoAG), represent the first coordinated, multi-sector approach to addressing the substantial health issues and other disadvantages our people experience. Progress will depend on sustained and appropriate resources with collaboration between Indigenous leaders and communities, the health sector and all levels of government.

Closing the gap

Virtually all of the indicators in the report *Overcoming Indigenous Disadvantage: Key Indicators 2016*, published by the Steering Committee for the Review of Government Service Provision, reveal wide gaps in the health of Indigenous and non-Indigenous Australians. In a few areas the gaps are narrowing; however, many other indicators show no improvement, or deterioration. This means the government still has

Courtesy of AIATSIS and Healing Foundation. Photographer: Andrew Turner

a considerable distance to travel to achieve the CoAG commitment to close the gap on Aboriginal and Torres Strait Islander disadvantage. The report also identifies the need for improved data.

Deaths in custody

In 1987 a Royal Commission investigated the social, cultural and legal issues involved in the deaths of Indigenous Australians while in police custody and prison. The 1991 Royal Commission into Aboriginal Deaths in Custody report provides harrowing reading. At that time, Aboriginal people made up 14 per cent of the total prison population and were up to fifteen times more likely to be in prison than non-Aboriginal Australians. Aboriginal deaths in custodial environments are still alarmingly high. To date, few of the report's recommendations have been carried out. The rate of Indigenous Australian deaths in prison custody in 2003 was

Indigenous prison and police custody rates have actually increased since the Royal Commission tabled its report. Photo courtesy of AAP/Richard Milnes

2.1 per 1,000 prisoners, compared to 1.6 per 1,000 non-Indigenous prisoners. The rates of Indigenous Australian deaths in prison custody peaked in 1995 and have been declining since.

The modest proposals of the report are designed to interrupt and reverse this insidious cycle. Strategies like mandatory sentencing will always disproportionately affect Aboriginal Australians, who are already over-represented in the criminal justice system.

EDUCATION

For tens of thousands of years our world view, spirituality and practical survival skills have been handed down to successive generations. Many of us understand the importance of a mainstream education for both our children's and our communities' benefit. More of our youth are completing Year 12 and going on to vocational or tertiary studies. The number of Indigenous 14 to 24-year-olds undertaking tertiary education has grown from 14.1 per cent in 2011 to 16.2 per cent in 2016.

Bilingual education

Bilingual education was used by missionaries in the Pitjantjatjara lands in northern South Australia in the 1940s. It

DID YOU KNOW?

Koori Courts exist in Victoria and New South Wales as an initiative to address high incarceration rates among young Aboriginal (Koori) men. The courts aim to address feelings of cultural alienation and account for cultural needs in sentencing. They aim to encourage offenders to appear in court, participate in the process, increase community awareness about the law and reduce re-offending. Court settings are informal, family members and elders can be present, and plain English is used to ensure defendants can understand the process.

spread to a few other communities and in the 1970s was introduced into Northern Territory remote government schools and a few schools in northern Queensland and outback Western Australia. Bilingual education' refers to teaching people to read and write in their mother tongue or first language for the first few years (see p. 45) and then switching to literacy and instruction in the national or mainstream language. In Australia, this is Standard Australian English. The reasoning behind this is that it is easier to learn to read and write in a second language if a person is literate in their first language.

Not everyone agrees with bilingual education. Some people believe Australian schools should be English-only all the way through. By the 1990s, Northern Territory schools had switched back to the English-only model, but some schools call themselves 'two-way' and still use a bilingual model. In 2009 the NT Government introduced a First Four Hours policy which requires schools to teach in English only in the vital first hours of school.

Class in Tjunjtjunjara community (WA). Photo: Indigenous Literary Foundation

Dr Misty Jenkins, Laboratory Head (Immunology), Walter and Eliza Hall Institute of Medical Research. Photo: Walter and Eliza Hall Institute of Medical Research, 2016

Gunditjmara woman and cancer researcher and immunologist, Misty Jenkins, said that when she was growing up a career in science was neither expected nor encouraged. However, Misty is passionate about the importance of Aboriginal and Torres Strait Islander perspectives in science:

> We're desperate for more Indigenous scientists... Indigenous people have had genetics for thousands of years — you know, not marrying within your own skin name and all that sort of stuff. So we need to have a voice there, we need to have a place.

Sometimes Australia's school curricula lacks interest and breadth. For example, Australian children should not learn that James Cook 'discovered' Australia. After all, the story is much more interesting and exciting than that — and we know we were already here! And the Macassans, Portuguese and others came to Australia long before him.

Batchelor Institute Senior Director of Alliance Management Dr Stephen Hagan with graduates Rakuwan and Hamish Gondarra. Photo: Darren O'Dwyer

The remote community of Yirrkala recently celebrated the achievements of forty graduates who have completed a range of courses at the Batchelor Institute of Indigenous Tertiary Education. The ceremony was the largest of its kind on record for Yirrkala, allowing students to celebrate their accomplishments with their friends and family in community rather than travel long distances to a graduation held on one of the main campuses in Darwin or Alice Springs. Students donned Batchelor Institute's yellow gowns and ochre sashes and many students also incorporated traditional headpieces and face-painting with their academic dress.

Among the Batchelor Institute graduates were father and daughter Hamish and Rakuwan Gondarra, who completed their Certificate II in Conservation and Land Management. Hamish is currently working as a ranger with the Dhimurru Aboriginal Corporation. During his studies he was also a part of the Learning on Country program, which sees rangers and elders contribute to the education of school students. Rakuwan was a Year 12 VET in Schools student, who completed her Year 12 certificate and the Certificate II in Conservation and Land Management, as well as becoming a mother.

The majority of students attained Certificates I and II in Conservation and Land Management to help in their current roles as rangers. Several students also completed a Certificate II in Resources and Infrastructure Work Preparation, as well as those who received certifications in Business, Training and Assessment and Aboriginal and Torres Strait Islander Health Care.

Certificates were presented by Dr Stephen Hagan, a Kullilli man, whose education journey is a remarkable story in itself. Dr Hagan was raised on a fringe camp on the outskirts of the small rural community, Cunnamulla, in far south-west Queensland and now holds an MBA and PhD from the University of Southern Queensland.

Sunset at Yellow Water Billabong, Kakadu National Park. Photo: Amity Raymont

Today, Australia's schools, universities and technological colleges are developing courses that acknowledge us as Aboriginal and Torres Strait Islander students, just as Australia has embraced and respected the European and Asian cultures of immigrant Australians.

Nearly every university around the country has an Aboriginal or Indigenous Australian studies centre that provides courses about Aboriginal and Torres Strait Islander lives and cultures. These centres also support Aboriginal and Torres Strait Islander students by helping with accommodation and other issues in adjusting to life as a tertiary student.

EMPLOYMENT

Depending on where we live, we have worked in dual economies: in natural resources, via hunting and gathering, and in the waged economy. Our people have been the labour backbone of the pastoral and pearling industries, particularly in northern Australia, although forced removals, dislocation, truncated education, racism, and so on have erected significant barriers to our employment.

Each region has its own particular mix of disadvantages, so the community and elders have an important role to play in planning remedial action. Our median income is just 35 per cent of those of non-Indigenous Australians. The median weekly gross personal income is up from $397 in 2011 to $441 in 2016. Although incomes grew generally between censuses, the growth in our incomes outpaced that of the rest of the population. Nevertheless, on average, we still receive a personal income that is only two-thirds that of the non-Indigenous population, so there is much to be done.

DID YOU KNOW?

Between 1900 and 1914 Australia provided between one-half and three-quarters of the world's supply of pearl shell, which was used for making buttons, ornaments and cutlery handles. Most of the pearl shell was sold to the United Kingdom.

Some communities have developed flourishing businesses, and the skills learnt in these enterprises have allowed people to begin other projects and take on further educational opportunities.

Successful enterprises

Enterprising Aboriginal and Torres Strait Islander communities and individuals have set up successful businesses across Australia. From Redfern to Gosford, Lakes Entrance to Eden, Adelaide to Perth, Oenpelli to Broome, and beyond, Indigenous enterprises are to be found in many industries and sectors including mining, catering, tourism industries, the arts, media and retail sectors, and in employment consultancies.

Individuals or families may have their own private businesses at various scales in art and craft and fashion, lawn mowing, photography and construction, to name just a few. These examples illustrate the diverse nature and size of our enterprises.

Other enterprises may be driven by the need for socio-economic security to be achieved by enabling community development, service provision and economic development. The Wathaurong community in Geelong offers property developers efficient services to deal with native title and heritage listings. This service provides employment, a climate of confidence for developers to proceed with their projects, and a positive relationship model for Indigenous and non-Indigenous Australians. The Wathaurong Aboriginal Co-operative's glass factory produces art which is sold internationally, with an internal focus on training artists, glass craftspeople and business managers. The success of the operation is a source of much pride and brings a sense of independence to the community.

Local employment initiatives run by Aboriginal and Torres Strait Islander organisations cover a wide range of activities in just about every area and industry. The Koonibba community at Ceduna runs a building organisation that does repairs and maintenance on housing stock. They employ several people in this capacity and have established share-farming opportunities as well.

Staff at Gilimbaa. Photo: Courtesy of Gilimbaa

Gilimbaa is a full-service creative agency specialising in strategic and connected communication. It is driven by the power and process of storytelling and the role this plays in the education and celebration of culture and community. Gilimbaa, which means 'today' in the language of the Wakka Wakka people of Central Queensland, won the Supply Connect Supplier of the Year 2015, and has done work for Qantas, the G20 Summit and Australia Post, among many others.

Harry Watson. Photo: James Fisher/Tourism Australia

Harry Watson is a Nyikina elder who runs camel treks out of Mount Anderson Station in the Kimberley, Western Australia. The camel tours are part of Kimberley Dreamtime Adventure Tours, which is owned by Jarlmadangah Burru community.

Some businesses are based on cultural activities. Around Bateman's Bay and Eden in New South Wales the local people are working oyster leases and produce outlets, continuing a long history of fishing for abalone.

Other enterprises may be the result of native title and land rights agreements between Traditional Owners and private corporations and governments. Increasingly, industry and Aboriginal and Torres Strait Islander groups are looking to options that build the local Indigenous economy through business and contract opportunities. Native title agreements may give rise to substantial benefits that are held in trusts

Burnie bean. Photo: The Jawun organisation.

The Jawun logo painted on a burnie bean from Cape York, painted by Traditional Owner Ivy Minniecon. The bean is in the palm of an Aboriginal partner, who is giving it to a secondee as a sign of friendship and connection.

and utilised for a range of outcomes including education, environment, health and other social investments.

Nyamba Buru Yawuru (NBY) is a not-for-profit company owned by the Yawuru native title holders of Broome through their corporate group structure. NBY has the responsibility to generate income from Yawuru's assets including land, community, social and cultural capital and is a key driver in the local Broome economy.

The Jawun organisation in Cape York is building enterprises through partnerships between governments, industries, philanthropic organisations and Indigenous communities. Broader in scope than the locally

Quenten Agius' multi-award-winning business Aboriginal Cultural Tours runs tours of the Narangga and Ngadjuri nations in the Yorke Peninsula and Mid North regions, South Australia. Photo: James Fisher/Tourism Australia

focussed NBY, Jawun aims to improve the lives of Indigenous Australian peoples across the country through supporting local initiatives.

Not all agreements involve significant financial benefit, many are focussed on non-monetary outcomes of key importance to local communities. Nevertheless, whatever shape and size, they almost all aim to strengthen and support local community, cultural values and identities.

A number of government initiatives and policies, such as the commercially focussed Indigenous Business Australia, aim to assist Aboriginal and Torres Strait Islander peoples in becoming economically independent through business and commercial ventures. The national Indigenous Procurement Policy encourages Commonwealth government agencies to preference Aboriginal and Torres Strait Islander business in their purchases and contracts. Supply Nation is a network of Indigenous-owned and controlled businesses, the first organisation to focus on Indigenous Australian supplier diversity. To fulfil targets in the

Adam Goodes. Photo: Courtesy of Australian of the Year Awards

I see the way forward for our people is education and it is earning [our] own wealth. And I find that Indigenous-owned businesses are hiring Indigenous people, which is also then creating more wealth in the communities.

We really need to promote the Indigenous-owned businesses out there in the community, because a lot of people might not know about them. They might not know the services that those businesses provide and how they can not only help their businesses but actually grow their business.

Adam Goodes, 2016

Indigenous Procurement Policy, government has mandated that buyers consult Indigenous Business Direct, Supply Nation's list of Indigenous Australian businesses, to access services.

Part of the exodus of Torres Strait Islander peoples to the mainland was due to the pearling industry winding down in the 1950s, and we needed to search for work elsewhere in order to support our families. Many of the men worked cutting cane, but as this was only seasonal work they sought jobs further afield. Torres Strait Islander men went as far as the Pilbara in Western Australia during the mining boom of the 1960s and 1970s seeking work. Some returned to their islands, others remained in their new homes and helped maintain their communities having obtained employment in other fields. Some found work on the railways, the top teams eventually being wooed to national and overseas projects, with a Torres Strait Islander team holding a world speed record for track construction by hand. On 8 May 1968, the team destroyed the previous world record of 4.6 kilometres of track by laying a massive 7 kilometres in just twelve hours. The materials used in the construction included 910 tons of rail and 13,000 sleepers. This feat remains a source of great pride and celebration in the Torres Strait.

War service

Legal exclusions and discriminatory policies prevented many Aboriginal and Torres Strait Islander men and women from serving in Australia's military forces. In the First World War there was a rule to recruit servicemen to the Australian Inland Forces who were 'substantially of European origin'. In the Second World War after 1942 when Australia was threatened with invasion, and Darwin and Broome were bombed, Aboriginal and Torres Strait Islander men and women were encouraged to enlist if they were of 'less than half-caste'. During the 1960s and 1970s, Indigenous Australian men and women were exempted from military service. Only in the late twentieth century were all formal barriers to Indigenous Australians entering the defence forces removed.

Australian Army Indigenous soldiers from NORFORCE (North-West Mobile Force) who graduated from the Army Indigenous Development Program stand together at the Darwin cenotaph after the unit's 35th anniversary Freedom of Entry march through the streets of Darwin on 13 August 2016. Photo Courtesy of the Department of Defence

Despite these barriers, many thousands of Aboriginal and Torres Strait Islander people were willing to serve for Australia, from the Boer War in 1899 to Afghanistan today. More than 1,000 Indigenous Australians served in the First World War, and more than 4,000 in the Second World War. At least 300 Indigenous Australians served in the Vietnam War. Yet when many returned to civilian life in Australia they were not treated equally. Some servicemen and women, especially in the Second World War, found on their return that they were ejected from hotels or denied employment, voting rights and benefits of returned service personnel because of their Indigeneity. This unfair treatment after military service inspired some Indigenous Australians and their non-Indigenous mates from the services to fight for equal rights and freedom from discriminatory laws and policies.

We have fought in every war in which Australia has been engaged and often with great distinction. Reg Saunders was the first Aboriginal commissioned officer and fought for his country in the Middle East,

Studio portrait of servicewoman Lance Corporal Kathleen Jean Mary (Kath) Walker (Oodgeroo Noonuccal), c.1942. Photo: Australian War Memorial

Oodgeroo Noonuccal was born Kathleen Jean Mary Ruska in 1920. A descendant of the Noonuccal people of Minjerribah (North Stradbroke Island), she was a switchboard operator in the Australian's Women's Army Service and went on to become an activist, poet, writer and educator.

North Africa, Greece, Crete and Papua New Guinea in the Second World War. Leonard Waters was Australia's only (known) Aboriginal fighter pilot in the Second World War. One of our well-known servicewomen is the poet and political activist Oodgeroo Noonuccal, also known as Kath Walker, who served in the Australian Women's Army Service as a telegraphist/radio operator and was promoted to lance corporal. These are just a few examples of the thousands of Aboriginal and Torres Strait Islanders who served in the Australian defence forces in conflicts for their country. Many more served in Vietnam and Korea, and then in Somalia, Serbia, Timor, Iraq and Afghanistan.

In the First World War, the 11th Light Horse Regiment became known as the 'Queensland Black Watch' after its force was increased in 1918 by 26 Aboriginal recruits, who went on to see active service in the Jordan Valley against the Turkish Army. The 5th Light Horse Regiment was another popular force among Aboriginal recruits.

During the Second World War, from 1942 more than 830 men enlisted in the Torres Strait Light Infantry Battalion. These soldiers patrolled the Torres Strait and undertook reconnaissance to Papua New Guinea. Their knowledge of local reefs was crucial in helping navigate the waters, and they played an important role in providing food for the thousands of troops stationed in the area. Aboriginal and Torres Strait Islander women also joined the forces during the Second World War and assisted as volunteers to support service bases across Australia's north, working as domestics, cooks and helping to build and clear airfields.

During the Second World War special units were established in northern Australia such as the Northern Territory Reconnaissance Unit and the Northern Australian Observer Unit. These units were made up mostly of Aboriginal and Torres Strait Islander people who were recognised for their skills as observers, trackers and their knowledge of country. These northern units paved the way for today's NORFORCE (North West Mobile Force), of which 60 per cent are Indigenous Australian.

DID YOU KNOW?

The Pilbara Regiment provides a surveillance network for the north-west. The motto of the Pilbara Regiment is Mintu wanta, which is a Western Desert Aboriginal phrase meaning 'always alert'. It is the first time that an Aboriginal language has been incorporated in an Australian Defence Force regimental crest.

Sergeant Norman Daymirringu and Lance Corporal Reggie Numamurdirdi at the Lone Pine Ceremony held at St John's Church, Glebe, NSW before departing Australia bound for Gallipoli. Photo: © Commonwealth of Australia, Department of Defence

OUR
ACHIEVEMENTS

Aboriginal and Torres Strait Islander peoples have made and continue to make major contributions in all fields of endeavour. Our success in sport has inspired new generations of Aboriginal and Torres Strait Islander people and has often provided opportunities for us to pursue success on an equal basis with other Australians. The energies of our artists and excitement about their work are recognised worldwide as among Australia's most distinctive cultural contributions. Our contemporary forms of art and performance express our unique world views and reflect our engagement with ever-growing audiences. Some of these views come from millennia of veneration for ancestral creation of the land, while others provide critical new perspectives on Australia's colonial experience. Like all artists and performers, our forms adapt and grow with new influences and experiences.

Each year the Deadly Awards celebrates our talents and achievements across a broad range of endeavours including, music, sport, the arts, health, education and community. Some of our previous awardees include Professor Pat Dudgeon for her work in health, Adam Goodes for his achievements in sport, and Henry 'Seaman' Dan for his contributions to the music industry.

MUSIC

Traditional Aboriginal music is a vocal art and songs may often be 'given' to singers by a Dreaming being, most commonly during dreams. A series of these songs, which may have many verses, tells a story of a Dreaming ancestor who sang as they travelled through the land. These songs are passed down from generation to generation and can help people live well on their land by describing water sources or places where plants or game are plentiful. People who are given the songs are the Traditional Owners of the land. These songs are proof of our continuous association with the land, an important requirement for land claims.

Songs like the Nyamal train song that was performed by Topsy Fazeldine in 1964 about the Pilbara steam train that ran between Marble

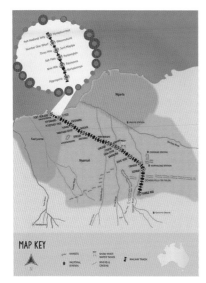

Top: The route of the Pilbara steam train. Map created by Monica Conaghan, AIATSIS. Top right: Opening of the Port Hedland–Marble Bar Railway. The Ministerial Train at Gorge Creek, 16 July 1911. Courtesy of the State Library of Western Australia 008368PD. Right: Topsy Fazeldine (Marrparingu) photographed in 1964 when she recorded the train song. Photo: AIATSIS Von Brandenstein Collection C03 CS-000169588

Bar and Port Hedland between 1911 and 1951 connect recent histories and experiences to ancient song styles. These songs are composed by individual song men or women for anyone to listen to. They are often accompanied by a rasp that gives the song rhythm. They are entertaining and poetic, and often name places in our landscape, forming a songline of knowledge as well as a story of an experience like travelling on a train, a truck or a boat.

Kelsey Barker, a musician from Tamworth, playing at the St George Hotel in rural Qld. Photo courtesy Kelsey Barker

Singer, composer and producer Jessie Lloyd rekindles another music tradition, travelling, recording and searching through archives for songs from the 1920s to 1970s about day to day life on the missions, settlements and reserves expressed through songs.

The popular band Yothu Yindi, from north-east Arnhem Land, combines traditional Yolngu melodies and words with modern pop and rock songs. One of their most widely recognised songs 'Treaty' includes both English and Yolngu languages and was the fifth biggest selling Australian song in the first year of its release. The song earned Yothu Yindi five ARIA Awards including Song of the Year. The group established the Yothu Yindi Foundation in 1990 to promote Yolngu cultural development from which the annual Garma Festival was born (see p. 183). A former member, Gumatj man Dr Gurrumul Yunupingu, became internationally renowned for his guitar playing and his songs in Yolngu-matha languages, bringing topics such as his Dreaming, culture and community to the world stage.

Jimmy Little from Cummeragunga on the Murray River in New South Wales sang 'Royal Telephone' on TV in the 1960s, and launched a long and illustrious career inspired by his parents. Many of our communities were sustained by songs like 'Nemeralla Pines', 'Yorta Yorta Man' and others that protested against the conditions faced by Aboriginal people.

Kev Carmody's 'From Little Things Big Things Grow' (co-written with Paul Kelly) might be a contemporary classic of popular modern music, but it has evolved directly from Aboriginal country music common on pastoral stations and in rural areas. Similarly, Archie Roach sang of 'Charcoal Lane' in inner-city Melbourne's Fitzroy, but the lament has its basis in the mission settlements of Framlingham and Lake Condah in country Victoria where he lived.

Troy Cassar-Daley, Kutcha Edwards, the Stiff Gins and many others are successful in the field of popular music. In a different field, Maroochy Barambah and Deborah Cheetham have become celebrated performers of Western classical music, following in the footsteps of the famous singer, Harold Blair (192476).

Cairns-born Torres Strait Islander, Christine Anu, originally trained as a dancer. Her 1995 debut album, *Stylin' Up*, included her version of the song 'My Island Home', written by Neil Murray and originally recorded by the Warumpi Band in 1986. That same year Murray won the 'Song of the Year' at the Australasian Performing Rights Association Awards.

The Warumpi Band, which takes its name from the Honey Ant Dreaming site near Papunya in the Northern Territory, developed a unique style of rock music. In 1983, the band members wrote, recorded and released the first rock song in an Aboriginal language, 'Jailanguru Pakarnu' ('Out of Jail'). It was voted one of the top ten recordings in the National Film and Sound Archive's listings, Sounds of Australia, in 2007.

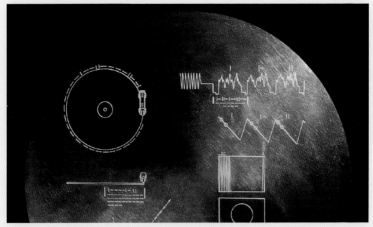

One of the golden records sent into space. Source: NASA

In 2013, NASA spacecraft Voyager I left our solar system with a golden record containing the aural heritage of earth on board. Part of this heritage included recordings of Milingimbi locals Mudpo, Djawa and Waliparu, singing 'Morning Star', a clan song relating to the *Barnumbirr morning star ceremonies*, and 'Mokoi', a song about the morkoi, malicious spirits who try and lure souls away from country.

Younger members of our community are drawing on musical influences from overseas and adapting them for their own purposes. While it emerged from the urban slums of the USA, hip hop found a new home in regional and remote communities and in the cities. Young Aboriginal men and women have taken hip hop music and made it their own, building on our oral culture heritage. Yorta Yorta hip hop artist, Briggs, is an Australian favourite with regular rotation on radio. Briggs won a

Briggs. Photo: Bad Apple Music

number of Australian awards and has supported international artists like Ice Cube and Ghostface Killah. As a multidisciplinary artist, Briggs is on your televisions starring in *Cleverman*, *Black Comedy*, *The Weekly with Charlie Pickering* and *Get Krackin*, as well as writing scripts for Matt Groening's new animation series, *Disenchantment*. His outspoken critiques of Australian culture have given a strong voice to Aboriginal and Torres Strait Islanders nationally.

Noongar people of southern Western Australia have taken the global phenomenon of karaoke and made it Noongaroke, public performances of resistance, humour and Noongar talk (Haebich & Morrison 2014).

Torres Strait Islanders have always been skilled absorbers and adaptors of the musical traditions of other people. By the end of 1872, one year after the London Missionary Society had arrived in the Torres Strait, hymns and choruses were being sung each day. In the early twentieth century, influential Anglo-American musical forms spread through the Torres Strait and met and merged with the music of the islands, which was being transformed by the sacred music of the South Sea Islander missionaries.

In the 1950s, Torres Strait Island music developed in another direction when the late Solkos Tabo, Weser Whaleboat, Sonny Kaddy and George Passi began composing songs in the style of Hawaiian Pan-Pacific songs which became the music for 'hula' concerts. At the same time, Thursday Islanders Seaman Dan and George Dewis were learning the songs of Nat King Cole and others. Competition between Torres Strait Islander composers was strong and the songs later became known as Kole Kabem Wed and replaced European music in the islands' dancehalls. Rock and roll arrived in the Torres Strait in the late 1960s with band leaders like Ritti Doolah. The Mills Sisters adopted church and popular music from their home islands to become successful performers throughout Australia, while singer Rita Mills has toured the world, sharing her music and culture.

> **DID YOU KNOW?**
>
> Cairns-based Torres Strait Islander cabaret singer, Georgia Lee (Dulcie Pitt), was part of the jazz and blues circuit in 1950s Sydney. She later pursued an overseas career and recorded the first album by an Indigenous Australian musician.

There are songs for all pastimes, from playing to boating, and songs to accompany sacred and secular dances. Traditionally, few musical instruments were used apart from the human voice and drums. Occasionally, percussion was added, a rattle, with Jew's harps, pan pipes and notched flutes providing the wind instruments. Today, these have been replaced by other instruments.

With the coming of local radio and, later, television, the unique Torres Strait Islander musical culture is less dominant than it used to be, though most of the music heard in the islands until the 1990s was locally composed. This music is still maintained in a lively way among the older generation and in the large groups of people who have moved away from the islands.

THEATRE AND DANCE

Dance is a vital expression of Aboriginal and Torres Strait Islander cultures, both as part of ceremonies and as entertainment. Body painting and a variety of paraphernalia, including headdresses, are associated with dance.

Many traditional dances depict incidents and activities from the Dreaming. Other dances tell stories about the land and the community and their relationships. Different communities tell their own stories; each group has its own distinct style of expression, and in some areas families pass down dances from one generation to the next. The best dancers are held in high esteem.

Some dances have their origins in the past, while others are more contemporary. For example, the Aeroplane Dance tells the story of a Second World War bomber that came down near Borroloola in the Northern Territory. Dancers mimic the flight of the aeroplane while performing the traditional stomping dance.

A more recent adaptation is by the Djuki Mala, whose 'Zorba the Greek Yolngu Style' has become a hit on YouTube. While they originally devised the dance just for fun, the young men now perform widely.

The Maya Wunba Dancers perform at Dance Rites, Sydney, 2017. Photo: Daniel Boud

A delighted audience at the 2017 Dance Rites competition watches the Maya Wunba Dancers perform. The dancers are from Cairns, far north Queensland and are representatives of the Djabugay Nation. Dance Rites is Australia's national Indigenous Australian dance competition which aims to ensure important cultural knowledge, including language, dance, skin-markings, and instruments, are shared from one generation to the next. It is held every year at the Sydney Opera House with over 300 dancers performing.

The Bangarra Dance Theatre is a leading modern dance company which has forged an international reputation for artistic innovation. Bangarra, a Wiradjuri word meaning 'to make fire', takes inspiration from Indigenous Australian cultures with each member in the group drawing on their own heritage.

The Saibai Dancers are especially known for their bow-and-arrow dances. The theatre production *Bran Nue Dae* and its music are true to the heart of the Broome area. Jimmy Chi and the Pigram Brothers

Beau Dean Riley Smith (right) performs in Bangarra Dance Theatre's *Bennelong* (2017). Photo: Daniel Boud

toured this very popular production throughout Australia which was subsequently made into a successful film in 2010 by Rachel Perkins.

Sydney and other major city audiences had the chance to learn Pitjantjatjara when they went to the theatre to see *Ngapartji Ngapartji* ('I give you something; you give me something'), which describes the Spinifex people's encounter with weapons testing at Woomera from 1953 to 1965 in remote South Australia.

Torres Strait Islanders adopted other influences in dance as well as music. The Taibobo songs and dances from the South Sea Island people were taught to many. Torres Strait Islanders soon began to compose their own Taibobo. Contemporary Torres Strait Island dance songs, such as Segur Kab Wed, date back to between 1900 and 1910. In the 1920s some of the best dancers from Badu, Moa, Yam and Murray Islands combined the traditional Kab-Kar and the newer Taibobo into

Keriba Mabaigal Dance Group perform. Photo courtesy of Black Drum Productions

one dance. This happened when a group of pearling luggers sailed to Mabuiag Island and the men held a dance workshop while seeking shelter from bad weather. 'Play Song' became part of that dance and it is now known widely in north Queensland and Papua as Segur Kaba Wed, meaning 'play dance and song'.

VISUAL ART

We have always been artists. We paint in rock shelters and caves, on our bodies for ceremony and in some regions we construct vast artworks on the ground as vital components of ritual. Rock paintings from the Kimberley's Carpenter's Gap have been dated at 40,000 years old, and the concentric circle art of central Australia is thought to be the oldest continuing art tradition in the world. We also paint on tools, shields and musical instruments.

Our artists make art for sale and the styles are as diverse as the cultures and histories of the artists. To teach outsiders about our spirituality we draw on ceremonial arts. The Aboriginal art movement at Papunya Tula grew out of ceremonial designs made on the ground, but now the artists paint huge canvasses for museums and

Reko Rennie, Kamilaroi/Gamilaraay/Gummaroi people, Message Stick (Green) 2011, hand-pressed textile foil, screen print on Belgium linen, 140.5 x 140.5 x 5 cm, National Gallery of Australia, Canberra, purchased 2012

galleries around the world. In Arnhem Land, intricate body-art ochre designs are now also painted on large pieces of flat bark, which are offered for sale, and many of which now hang in art galleries.

Emily Kame Kngwarreye and Kathleen Petyarre of Utopia, Clifford Possum Tjapaltjarri of Papunya, Rover Thomas of Warmun and Banduk Marika of Yirrkala are internationally renowned: all are artists who participated in ceremony and used that experience as inspiration in their creation of contemporary art.

Hermannsburg, where the famous painter Albert Namatjira first worked, is nowadays also a major location for women's decorated ceramics.

Reko Rennie is a Kamilaroi/Gamilaraay/Gummaroi man, born in Melbourne, Australia in 1974. Through his art, Reko explores what it means to be an urban Aboriginal man in contemporary Australian society. Rennie received no formal artistic training but as a teenager discovered graffiti, which would become an all-consuming passion. He quickly began producing original art on the streets of Melbourne. His art and installations continually explore issues of identity, race, law and justice, land rights, the Stolen Generations and other issues affecting Aboriginal and Torres Strait Islanders in contemporary society. Rennie was shortlisted for the 2012 Archibald Prize for his portrait of curator Hetti Perkins.

Yvonne Koolmatrie lives in the Riverland region and makes innovative sculptures and traditional fishtrap forms in fibre using coil-weaving techniques learnt from Shirley Trevorrow. Victorian Aboriginal artists Vicki Couzens, Treahna Hamm and Lee Darroch have revived the art of decorating possum-skin cloaks. While at Ernabella, Jillian Davey and others work in new techniques of batik and print-making, and the colours and designs relate to their experience of country.

A necklace of opalescent green maireener (rainbow kelp) shells and black crows shells made by Lola Greeno of Tasmania. Photo: AIATSIS collection R01630-ATS 77

Judy Watson, *fire and water*, 2007, 46 x 6 x 3.7 m, bronze, granite, steel, reeds and sound piece. Reconciliation Place, Canberra. Sound: Michael Hewes. Urban Art Projects. © the artist. Courtesy the artist and Milani Gallery, Brisbane

> The metal bower is suggestive of a bower bird's 'avenue' and of the skeletal supports of a shelter. The way the forms bend towards each other is a gesture of reconciliation and understanding, a listening space. The passage through the bower is a metaphysical journey, reflecting on the land and the culture of the Traditional Owners of this space, the Ngunnawal and the Ngambri people. It is a coming together of black and white, a welcoming, sheltering, reflective space. All who live, work, or visit here are walking together, respectful of each other's culture and of being together on the same ground.

Judy Watson

Others have drawn on their urban experiences to create art in new formats including photography and film, as well as sculpture, jewellery-making and painting in new materials. Photographer, curator

Raymond Zada, Kamilaroi/Wiradjuri peoples, 'racebook' 2012, Giclée print, 50 x 150 cm, National Gallery of Australia, Canberra, purchased 2012

Raymond Zada, a South Australian artist, used the contents of the Facebook groups 'Aboriginal Spongebob' and 'Giving ya wife a sniff of ya petrol cos ur a top noonga' to create racebook. Zada, who is of Aboriginal, Afghan and Scottish descent, made up the word racebook using the site's racial slurs, in a style that references the Facebook logo.

and academic Bronwyn Croft's autobiographical, evocative works are held in major public and private collections in Australia and overseas. Waanyi artist Judy Watson's etched zinc panels are celebrated in many public buildings in Australian cities.

Tasmanian artists like Dulcie Greeno, Patsy Cameron and Lola Greeno are teaching shell necklace-making, basketry and working with kelp to a younger generation of artists. Denis Nona, from Badu Island, was taught traditional woodcarving techniques that he translated into intricate linocuts. He has also been encouraged to interpret creation stories in bronze sculptures, and he and Alick Tipoti's art is now exhibited internationally. Ken Thaiday Snr, a Torres Strait Islander artist living on the mainland, has developed elaborate headdress sculptures based on the themes of traditional dances. Richard Bell and Destiny Deacon provide sharp comments on issues of sexism, racism, and the place of Aboriginal arts in contemporary Australia, in

Alick Tipoti is an artist from Badu Island in the Torres Strait. His rooftop installation *Turtle mating and nesting season* covered the roof of the Oceanographic Museum of Monaco as part of the *Taba Naba — Australia, Oceania, Arts of the Sea People* exhibition in 2016. Photo: Michel Dagnino

their images and installations. Photographer Michael Riley grew up in Dubbo and was a founding member of the Boomalli Aboriginal Artists Cooperative in Sydney.

Artists' work is often sold through community-owned organisations, but we also license our artworks to others, and the images we produce can be found on a range of clothes and other objects.

Each year our talent in the arts is celebrated at the Red Ochre Awards and the annual Telstra National Aboriginal and Torres Strait Islander Art Award. Originally intended as a celebration for our own communities, these events are fast making their mark on the wider arts scene. Those responsible for our art in the galleries of capital cities around the country regularly organise large exhibitions featuring a range of art forms.

INDIGENOUS ART CODE

The Indigenous Art Code is a system to preserve and promote ethical trading in Indigenous Australian art. The Code supports the rights of Aboriginal and Torres Strait Islander artists to negotiate fair terms for their work and gives buyers greater certainty about an artwork's origin. Dealers who are Code signatories have agreed to comply with the Code's ethical standards in their dealings with Indigenous Australian artists and with art buyers. They may display the Code logo and apply Code certificates to artworks to demonstrate this commitment.

FILM AND TELEVISION

Television and film have become home to some of our most celebrated artists. Deborah Mailman, Leah Purcell, David Gulpilil, Ernie Dingo, Luke Carroll and Aaron Pederson and many others, appear regularly on our cinema and television screens. Trisha Morton-Thomas is a well-known Aboriginal actor, writer and producer, who has starred and written several works. She is best known for her roles in *Radiance*, and *Redfern Now I* and *II*, as well as writing, producing and starring in the hilarious *8MMM Aboriginal Radio*, and the important documentary, *Occupation: Native*. Films like *Radiance*, *BabaKiueria* and *Utopia* have reached mainstream audiences, while Warwick Thornton's *Samson & Delilah*, Ivan Sen's *Toomelah*, Brett Charles' *Ailan Kastom* and Beck Cole's *I Am Here*, have provided unflinching, contemporary insider visions of Aboriginal and Torres Strait Islander lives.

Frances Peters-Little, a Kamilaroi-Uralari film-maker and academic, won a Sundance Award for her film *Tent Embassy* and has produced documentaries for the ABC. Richard Frankland has also made documentaries, and his 2007 film *Convincing Ground*, explored the legal battle by Gunditjmara people to prevent development on a massacre site in Portland, Victoria. The television series *Remote Area Nurse* was filmed on Masig Island in the Torres Strait and gave viewers insights into the work of nursing in remote communities, as well as the contemporary lives of Torres Strait Islanders.

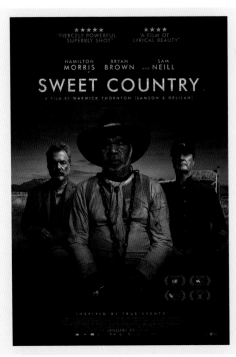

Warwick Thornton's *Sweet Country*, a period western set in 1929 in the Northern Territory, follows a journey of personal conviction and settler justice with Thornton's central themes of colonialism, law, and power. *Sweet Country* won the 2017 Venice Film Festival's Special Jury Prize and is the 2017 Toronto Film Festival's Platform Winner.

101

The ABC series *Black Comedy* infuses the tradition of sketch comedy with the unique sense of humour most Indigenous Australian peoples claim. Its sketches are witty and incisive critiques of the nation's race relations, balanced with a deep love for Aboriginal and Torres Strait Islander peoples and cultures.

Popular television show *Cleverman* tells the story of an Indigenous superhero, combining sci-fi, fantasy, politics, and Aboriginal spirituality and history. Creator Ryan Griffen came up with the series because he wanted his son to have an Indigenous

Singer and actor Jessica Mauboy. Photo courtesy of Sony Music

Australian superhero. Directed by Wayne Blair and Leah Purcell the show has a cast that is over 80 per cent Indigenous Australian.

LITERATURE

Like our film-makers and artists, there are many award-winning and ground-breaking Aboriginal and/or Torres Strait Islander writers: Melissa Lucashenko, Anita Heiss, Terri Janke, Vivienne Cleven, Jared Thomas, Samuel Wagan Watson, Ellen van Neerven, Paul Collis, Philip McLaren, Tony Birch and John Clarke just to name a few. These authors work mostly in English using the modern styles and challenging the status quo, especially in fiction and poetry. In 2000, Kim Scott became the first Aboriginal person to win Australia's most prestigious writing prize, the Miles Franklin Award, for his book, *Benang*. He repeated this amazing feat in 2011 with his work, *That Deadman Dance*. In 2007, Alexis Wright also won the Miles Franklin for her work, *Carpentaria*.

Melissa Lucashenko.
Photo: Mark Crocker

Melissa Lucashenko's *Mullumbimby* is a good example of how First Nations writers are infusing Australian languages into their writings, in this case the Yugambeh-Bundjalung language. *Mullumbimby* won the fiction category of the Queensland Literary Awards in 2013. Melissa is of Goorie and European heritage.

Some of our writers leave us in no doubt that their stories are unique and from the strong tradition of storytelling within our communities. Wright's *Carpentaria* is an epic work that captures and celebrates the country, culture and political battles of her people. These writers draw on the literary heritage provided by acclaimed literary forebears like Jack Davis, Kevin Gilbert and Oodgeroo Noonuccal. Steve Kinnane's *Shadow Lines* uses Western Australian government and police records to plot the course of Australia's assimilationist approach, which assumed our cultures would die out and we would simply be absorbed into the culture of the colonisers.

Ngarrindjeri writer and inventor David Unaipon is today celebrated as the first published Aboriginal author after he was commissioned by the University of Adelaide to assemble a book on Indigenous Australian stories in the early 1920s. His novel was stolen from him and published with heavy edits as, *Myths and Legends of the Australian Aboriginals*, written by W Ramsay Smith. This terrible injustice was finally corrected in 2006 when Melbourne University Press worked to publish the work under Unaipon's name as *Legendary Tales of the Australian Aborigines*. David Unaipon was also the first Aboriginal writer to be published in the English language, with a number of his articles in the *Sydney Daily Telegraph* discussing Aboriginal rights, traditional customs and even his inventions.

We began writing soon after the colonisers introduced this form of communication to the country. From the early days of the colonies, we adopted and used it for our own ends. Bennelong's letter of 1796 was dictated to a scribe, but soon after we took printed objects and written papers beyond the frontiers of colonisation. Some were assimilated into our graphics and social life, and by the 1930s and 1940s the Palawa people of Tasmania, among others, were creating subversive

The Australian $50 note features David Unaipon.

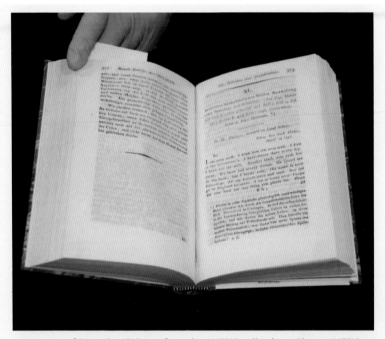

A rare copy of Bennelong's letter from the AIATSIS collections. Photo: AIATSIS Collections

The AIATSIS Collection holds a very precious copy of what is considered to be the first known use of written English by an Aboriginal Australian. It is a copy of what is known as the 'Bennelong Letter' and represents a seminal work in Australian Aboriginal literature. It is also the first time that an Aboriginal author has appeared in print. Woollarawarre Bennelong was a Wangal man from the south shore of the Parramatta River, who is believed to have been born about 1764. Governor Arthur Phillip kidnapped him and another person in 1789, believing that teaching them European ways would somehow build relations between the different peoples and cultures. Eventually they formed a friendship and in 1972 Phillip took Bennelong and his kinsman Yemmerrawanne to England.

Dr Josie Douglas holding the glass eel-trap trophy (designed by Jennifer Kemarre Martinello) for the 2017 Stanner Award for an academic manuscript by an Indigenous Australian writer, which she won for her PhD thesis 'Kin and Knowledge: the meaning and acquisition of Indigenous Ecological Knowledge in the lives of young Aboriginal people in Central Australia'. Photo: AIATSIS

versions of the Bible, as well as writing sermons, community newspapers and letters to colonial authorities. People from Lake Condah and Coranderrk in Victoria wrote letters to the government complaining of conditions on the missions and stations, and many other areas used writing in their own ways. These letters and others are part of a resistance to white control of our lives that has endured.

Today not only do we have acclaimed writers working in many areas of literature, but there are also a growing number of Aboriginal and

Torres Strait Islander academics whose works are making important contributions to their respective fields.

The *Indij Readers For Big Fullas* and *Little Fullas* series of children's books were created to foster and increase children's literacy in the primary education system. North Queensland's Black Ink Press produces a range of children's books, some of which have been used in the accelerated literacy program in the Northern Territory and Western Australia. We have our own publishing houses too, including Magabala Books in Broome, the Institute for Aboriginal Development (IAD Press) in Alice Springs, and Aboriginal Studies Press (part of AIATSIS) in Canberra.

MEDIA

Indigenous Australian newspapers, notably the *Koori Mail*, the *National Indigenous Times* and the *Torres News*, play a pivotal role in communicating Aboriginal and Torres Strait Island current events, culture, politics and sport, as do radio programs like the ABC's *Message Stick*, *Speaking Out*, *Awaye!* and SBS TV's *Living Black*.

Attendees of the 2017 Remote Indigenous Media Festival, held in Wingellina, WA. Photo courtesy of IRCA

National Indigenous Television (NITV) aims to inform, entertain, educate, preserve our languages, tell our stories and showcase the rich diversity of our cultures and creative talent. The Central Australia Aboriginal Media Association includes an independent music label, film, television and radio broadcasting and production. Imparja is a commercial service in remote areas that broadcasts radio and television programs via satellite across more than 3.6 million square kilometres. The Indigenous Remote Communications Association (IRCA) is the peak body for Aboriginal and Torres Strait Islander broadcasting, media and communications.

Our writers, artists and musicians often combine their art with service to their community and, although this means less time for creative work, their connections to family and community are crucial ingredients of their work.

SPORT

We have always played sports. Sports and games were essential to living a good life and were played with sticks and with balls made from kangaroo and possum skins long before Europeans arrived. When traditional games could not be played any more our old people transferred some of the purposes and meanings on to the games introduced by Europeans. That gave the European games new meanings and resulted in our own distinct way of playing them.

Our athletes are powerful symbols of who we are. Generations of them have excelled at sports. Names such as Charlie Samuels, Eddie Gilbert, Lynch Cooper, Lionel Rose, Faith Thomas, Graham Farmer, Evonne Goolagong, Darby McCarthy, Arthur Beetson, the Krakouers, Riolis, Sands, Mundines and the Ellas are all sporting legends. Young Australians admire and hope to be the next Cathy Freeman, Cyril Rioli, Jonathan Thurston, Lance Franklin, Kyah Simon or Patrick Mills. Our athletes sometimes take advantage of the attention they receive to advocate for a 'fair go' for our people. Nicky Winmar, Michael Long,

Australian Aboriginal domestic scene depicting traditional recreation, including one child kicking a ball, with the object and caption being to 'never let the ball hit the ground'. From William Blandowski's *Australien in 142 Photographischen Abbildungen*, 1857 (Haddon Library, Cambridge).

Nova Peris, Anthony Mundine, Timana Tahu and Adam Goodes were and are champion athletes who became heroes when they bravely drew people's attention to prejudice, racism and inequality.

Kyah Simon is an Australian professional soccer striker who plays for Melbourne City in the Australian W-League and the Australian national Soccer team, the Matildas. In 2011, Simon became the first Indigenous Australian player to score a goal in a FIFA World Cup. Simon's mother is an Anaiwan woman and her father a Biripi man.

One awful stereotype that still exists today is the idea that Aboriginal and Torres Strait Islander people use some kind of

Members of the Gumatj clan added a red V and the no. 37 to their traditional paint as a show of support for Adam Goodes at Garma 2015 in northeast Arnhem Land. *Courtesy Melanie Faith Dove/Yothu Yindi Foundation*

inherited or magical sporting ability. This completely ignores the hard work and training that people put in to excel at their chosen sport. Instead of seeing our athletes as examples of good things about us and our communities, people too often see sport as confirming that our communities are places that we need to escape. It is not true that our communities are terrible places. Aboriginal people excel at sport because of, not in spite of, our communities. In fact, our communities are places that nurture sporting talent.

Sport may be the most important cultural field for future generations of Aboriginal and Torres Strait Islander peoples. Efforts by schools to revive and maintain traditional games will contribute to the type of cultural resurgence that is essential to our health and well-being.

Tribal Warrior II. Photo: SBS

The crew of the Tribal Warrior II, the first Indigenous Australian team to enter and complete the Sydney to Hobart Yacht Race. The team was made up of fifteen members from La Perouse, Redfern and the Central Coast, with a mix of Indigenous and non-Indigenous Australian crew members.

The Indigenous Marathon Foundation (IMF) coach Adrian Dodson-Shaw, Maletta Seriat, Scott Cox, Natasha Leslie and IMF founder and director Rob de Castella at the finish line of the New York City Marathon, November 2017. Photo: IMF

OUR
SHARED
HISTORY

As a nation, Australia suffers because it has never come to terms with the fact that an entire continent was taken from the Aboriginal and Torres Strait Islander peoples. Too few Australians are able to examine our shared colonial past seriously without averting their gaze from the unpalatable facts. Other countries have a better record of handling the tensions and differences of opportunity between their Indigenous and non-Indigenous peoples.

Since European colonisation began in 1788, we have responded to attempts to oppress us by using a range of strategies. Over time, depending on the circumstances and degree of governmental control, we have resisted, accommodated, worked towards reconciliation or combined these activities. Many among us still call ourselves activists, though our forms of activism have changed with the times.

EARLY RESISTANCE

In the contact period of Aboriginal Australian history, we often opposed the European colonisers by engaging in guerrilla warfare: small and swift attacks against a heavily armed invader. Early colonial newspapers were quick to label such hit-and-run tactics as 'treacherous' and colonial authorities declared martial law.

Nineteenth-century historians and commentators described large-scale frontier conflict, rather than an occasional skirmish. Henry Melville, in *The History of Van Diemen's Land 1824–1835*, commented that Aboriginal people were 'massacred without mercy...they were slaughtered in cold blood'. 'The historian,' he said, 'must ever lament, that he has to record outrages so inhuman and so unjust on the part of a British community'. John West's *History of Tasmania* (1852), while not critical of colonisation itself, provided extended and detailed accounts of white brutality. GW Rusden's *History of Australia* (1897) and Ernest Scott's popular *A Short History of Australia* (1916) noted the 'sheer brutality and treacherous murder by white settlers and their convict servants'.

Dr Keryn Walshe, South Australian Museum, with descendants of the massacre at Sturt Creek. Photo Courtesy of Dr Pam Smith

Aboriginal elders from the Kutjungka region of WA have passed on oral histories of the 1922 Sturt Creek Massacre, where more than a dozen of their ancestors were killed. These oral histories have been supported by a team of archaeologists and forensic scientists in the Flinders University-led study that was funded by an AIATSIS Research grant to the Kimberley Land Council and lead researcher, Dr Pam Smith.

Our various systems of organisation and control, established over thousands of years, were devised to best meet our needs. Traditionally, our governance is characterised by systems of land tenure that in some areas means descent group membership or in others relationship to Country by birth (as in the land a person was literally born on), added to which is the complex systems of shared responsibility derived from the Dreaming. This regional division of responsibility was reflected in our response to colonial invasion after 1788, which was conducted at a strictly local level against individual transgressors. It was not until the early 1810s in Tasmania (then in 1830s in New South Wales and 1840s in Victoria) that pan-Aboriginal resistance across local groups was organised.

Our forces were weakened by a combination of factors. In the late 1800s, we faced increasing numbers of British military forces and their advanced weaponry, coupled with raids by the Native Police, while also suffering dramatic losses of life from disease and warfare, a situation not helped by our reduced access to shelter and food.

Often the settlers fought the war outside the law and were rarely brought before the courts to account for their actions. Following the Myall Creek massacre in New South Wales in 1838, where at least twenty-eight Wirrayaraay people were killed by twelve armed stockmen, the perpetrators were tried before a court and seven were convicted and sentenced to death. Such was the outcry from the general public, that white men had been charged and found guilty of murdering Aboriginal people, that the authorities were reluctant to allow such cases to be tried before courts again. Nearly two hundred years later, the area was proclaimed a national heritage site.

> **DID YOU KNOW?**
>
> In 1830 a million acres of land was granted to settlers on the island of Van Diemen's Land, which fuelled one of the most violent conflicts in Australia's history. The Aboriginal survivors were interned on Flinders Island, including Trugermanner (Truganini), who was wrongly called 'the last Tasmanian Aborigine'. The Flinders Island community continues to hand down their culture and history to this day.

At Coniston in the Northern Territory in 1928 at least thirty-one people were killed in reprisal for the murder of Fred Brooks, a dingo trapper who was killed because of his mistreatment of a Warlpiri woman. Many believe the number of dead was closer to one hundred. The police officer who led the massacre was exonerated. In every state and territory the authorities and courts went to elaborate lengths to protect perpetrators of violence against us.

The methods of dispossession used in Australia were at different times spontaneous and a calculated campaign. Many of the men involved in implementing them had undertaken similar acts of dispossession in India, Africa and America. As part of the process of dispossession, it was useful to portray our people as a lesser branch of the human family, who neither 'tilled the soil' nor 'worked'. We came to be regarded by the colonists as people living off the land rather than producers — a self-serving myth perpetuated by settlers greedy for land, to which parliaments, courts and media still contribute today.

Introduced diseases like syphilis and influenza that came to Australia with the colonists took a significant toll on our populations. However, some theorists who consider disease to be the major cause of our population decline may be discounting the extent to which violence on the frontier had an impact on our numbers, and the lack of reporting that happened.

In the Torres Strait in the 1860s, European vessel masters sought trepang and trochus shell. Their crews included South Sea Islanders and later, Filipinos and Japanese people. Vast quantities of pearl shell were discovered in the 1870s and more ships arrived. Armed with guns, some of the crew members were able to overwhelm the Torres Strait Islanders. Some of them were safer than others, but women were abducted, gardens raided and men co-opted for work.

In 1871 the London Missionary Society landed two missionary teachers on Erub (Darnley) Island, and soon all the islands had been visited by missionaries. By the end of the decade communities without

The Missionary landing site memorial on Sabai Island. Photo: AIATSIS collection MACDONALD.G01.CS-000077478

missionary teachers were asking for them. Historians believe that this was in part because Christian beliefs were already compatible with the Torres Strait Islanders beliefs, but also because there was a belief that the missionaries could protect them from the violent acts of foreign seamen. The new religion was quickly accepted and absorbed, and for nearly forty years the London Missionary Society maintained strong control in the Torres Straits, though they were never able to force the Torres Strait Islanders to give up their traditional culture and beliefs.

The Queensland Government's annexation of some islands in 1872, and the remainder in 1879, was prompted more by fear of rival colonial powers and a desire to control the increasingly lucrative marine industry than to protect the people living there. The role of Government Resident was created, and the Honourable John Douglas was appointed to be responsible for the Torres Strait Islanders, among other duties. He remained in this job for eighteen years, a period marked by his easy-going brand of paternalism. When he died in 1904, the Chief Protector placed the Torres Strait Islanders under the same controls as Aboriginal people on the mainland. Queensland's native affairs policy was still emerging, but it was later to become a model for the rest of Australia. Two of its elements were extended instruction, while keeping us socially isolated from European society, and producing obedient unskilled workers. The *Torres Strait Islander Act 1939* followed, with further legislation in 1965, 1971 and 1979, 1984 and 1985.

PROTECTION ACTS

At a time of increasing democratic reforms for the non-Indigenous population, like the extension of franchise and free public education, Protection Acts were passed in every state except Tasmania following Victoria's Aboriginal Protection Act in 1869. These served to control and constrain Aboriginal lives, and amendments over the following years made them increasingly restrictive. They operated until the second half of the twentieth century, controlling the lives of Aboriginal and Torres Strait Island people. By 1881, New South Wales had an Aboriginal Protector and later a Board for the Protection of Aborigines.

DID YOU KNOW?

Tasmania was the only state not to enact protection legislation. It did not recognise that there were any Aboriginal peoples left after the Black Wars and the removal of Tasmanian Aboriginal people to Flinders Island in the first half of the nineteenth century.

A new law in 1915 gave the Board the right to assume control and custody of Aboriginal children and to remove them to 'such care and control as it thinks best' (see the Stolen Generations p. 126). In 1940, the New South Wales Board was reorganised into the Aborigines Welfare Board, which controlled Aboriginal lives in the state until 1969. The Board had a high degree of control and the ability to force us to do things, but offered us much less welfare and protection than we had under earlier arrangements.

RESERVES, STATIONS AND MISSIONS

Aboriginal people were desperately trying to scratch out a living as we were moved off our country and had little access to our usual bush foods and water sources. We had to rely instead on rations distributed by missions, the managers of government reserves and pastoralists, and we were often accused by colonists of stealing basic items like flour, sheep and clothes. Some colonists were concerned simply for the loss of their possessions; others were disturbed by our obvious distress. In the Torres Strait, too, we were subjected to controls over our movement. Colonial governments reacted in different ways. Most created reserves (areas of land) onto which we were moved, often taking us away from our country, our sources of food, our sacred sites and our families. Torres Strait Islanders were placed under curfews and had to obtain permits in order to travel. Chief Protectors were appointed, usually senior bureaucrats who, in turn, appointed other local protectors, usually missionaries and police, and their powers were wide-ranging. The Protector took control of people's earnings and we had to seek permission to access our own money, if we were paid at all, which many of us weren't. We adapted to these changes and engaged in agricultural pursuits such as growing hops and establishing craft industries. Many of us had some freedom of movement in the early days and were able to work, but the laws were changed over time, restricting our abilities to travel and control our own lives. All of the laws were designed to strengthen state and territory government control over us, and all of the acts enabled the removal of children, especially those of mixed descent (see the Stolen Generations, p. 126).

Missions were created with the aim of 'Christianising and civilising' Aboriginal people. Depending on the place and the people in charge, some of them were relatively benign, but in many the treatment was physically, emotionally and mentally abusive and authoritarian. Those in charge were often contemptuous of us. For example, in some cases women had to apply in writing to the mission

United Aborigines Mission, Ooldea, South Australia, 1939. The mission was established at Ooldea Soak in 1933. In 1939 the government established an Aboriginal reserve that encompassed the mission. A sixty-bed children's dormitory was established as part of the mission. Photo: AIATSIS collection MATHEWS.W01.DF-D00027950

superintendent if they needed underwear. The mission would then choose and make the purchase out of the women's own money. The Western Australian protection system, under AO Neville, was particularly destructive in its interference in even the most ordinary and private aspects of our lives.

In the Torres Strait, the government sought to define and contain people. Some of it was similar to what was happening in Aboriginal Australia. Europeans held positions of power in industry, commerce, government, religion and the military, while non-Europeans were subordinated but divided into two further groups: Torres Strait

People's race determined the seating arrangements at the Sun Pictures in Broome, WA, 1953. Photo: State Library of Western Australia, 010834D

Islanders and foreigners. Special laws prevented Japanese divers from moving up in society, and the government controlled Torres Strait Islanders' earnings and employment, while other divers dealt directly with their employers.

We weren't allowed in some public venues including swimming pools (see Freedom Rides, p. 155), whilst in other places we were only allowed in certain areas. For example, we could only go in one area of a pub, if we were allowed in at all, or had to sit in segregated areas of cinemas and buses. We were not able to travel freely and were made to live apart, while being offered fewer health and educational opportunities than non-Indigenous people.

Stations and reserves

Aware of the effects of violence, diseases and removal from our land, the colonial government believed that we were doomed to extinction. Part of the aim of the Aboriginal Protection Acts was so that Indigenous

Australians could be looked after during their remaining years. Aboriginal Protection Boards created reserves on which stations were often established and were managed by officials appointed by the boards. People on the reserves were regarded as wards of the state, with members of the Protection Boards as their legal guardians. While protection may have been the main aim of the acts, in practice the boards were given complete power and control over the lives of the Aboriginal people under their care.

The success of the stations varied according to the financial support they received and the personalities of their directors. Coranderrk in Victoria, for example, was a productive and economically stable station until government policy changed and it was disbanded.

Actors re-enact the 1881 Victorian Parliamentary Inquiry into the Corranderk Aboriginal Reserve. Photo: James Henry *CORANDERRK* and ILBIJERRI Theatre Company

Actors in Ilbijerri theatre's production of *CORANDERRK*, a play that re-enacts a Victorian Parliamentary Inquiry in 1881, where the men and women of the Coranderrk Aboriginal Reserve went head to head with the Aboriginal Protection Board. Their goal was both simple and revolutionary: to be allowed to continue the brilliant experiment in self-determination they had pioneered for themselves on the scrap of country left to them. The Coranderrk story was only recently unearthed and the play published in 2013.

Some reserves operated as prisons. Much has been written about Moore River Settlement in Western Australia, for example. Children were separated from their families and lived in dormitories. Those thought to be acting badly were placed in 'The Boob', a prison within a prison. Escape was difficult. The grandmother of Aboriginal activist Rob Riley spent almost twenty-five years in Moore River, because if she left she would have been required to leave her children behind.

Stories from Palm Island in north Queensland have shocked many with their examples of violence and brutality, especially by police. A physically beautiful place, Palm Island was originally established as a prison. A mixture of people who didn't share the same language and culture were sent there for minor offences. In 2004 media attention was drawn to the island following the death in custody of Mr Doomadgee. A coronial inquest followed and despite the original enquiry ruling that the arresting officer, Senior Sergeant Hurley, caused the injuries, a jury later found him not guilty of manslaughter. Early in 2010 another inquest into Mr Doomadgee's death was opened with the coroner handing down an open finding — meaning he was unable to make a definitive ruling.

> **DID YOU KNOW?**
> Cathy Freeman's grandfather was sent to Palm Island because he refused to sign an employment agreement, something he wasn't required to do. Cathy Freeman's mother, a generation later, requested permission to leave Palm Island to spend Christmas with her family in Cherbourg. She was refused.

The influence of the Church

In the Torres Strait, the Christian Church became closely integrated with our daily lives as the Christian calendar coincided with our seasonal calendar: Christmas was turtle season, Lent the 'hungry time', Easter was crop season. The Church also provided a hierarchy for men, from

All Saints Anglican Church on Erub (Darnley) Island. Photo © National Trust of Queensland (NTQDS13673)

The birthplace of Christianity in the Torres Strait. Hilly volcanic Erub Island was the place where the first Christian service in the Torres Strait took place. A bamboo church was the first building. This Romanesque style building, 1015 m from Badog Beach, went up in about 1890, and consists of timber framing, coral cement and a red corrugated asbestos cement (fibro) roof. The Coming of the Light festival is centred annually on this building. The festival marks the day the London Missionary Society first arrived in the Torres Strait. The missionaries landed at Erub Island on 1 July 1871, introducing Christianity to the region.

new parishioner to established churchgoer, to perhaps a deacon or pastor. In the 1890s, the responsibility for law and order, previously given to mamooses, someone acting as a chief and given power by the authorities, by a Queensland magistrate on the advice of a missionary, Samuel McFarlane, then passed to the government teacher.

125

> ## DID YOU KNOW?
>
> Bishop Kawemi Dai was the first Torres Strait Islander Anglican bishop. He was consecrated in 1986 on Thursday Island in a service which combined Anglican and traditional elements. In 2002, Meriam Bishop Saibo Mabo was consecrated as national bishop to the Torres Strait Islander peoples.

THE STOLEN GENERATIONS

The removal of children from their families was systematic and pervasive throughout the protection and assimilation policy eras. Across Australia, anywhere from one-in-three to one-in-ten children were removed from their families between 1910 and 1970, leaving one or more generations in most Aboriginal and Torres Strait Islander families affected by the forcible removal of children (HREOC 1997, p. 31).

Children were taken away from their families and placed in foster homes or institutions such as the Kinchela Boys Home, where they were treated like prison inmates.

The Human Rights and Equal Opportunity Commission (HREOC) Inquiry into the separation of Aboriginal and Torres Strait Islander children from their families was published in the *Bringing Them Home* report (1997). It detailed the laws, policies and practices that allowed our children to be taken from their families, and included many case studies that contest the claim made by many non-Indigenous Australians that the removal of our children was in their own interests.

The exact number of children who were removed may never be known, but the impact of the removals has traumatised our communities. Very few families have been left unaffected — in some families children from three or more generations were taken. Almost all of us have had a relative, including close family members, damaged by this policy. Some children were deeply affected by this sudden separation

The Kinchela boys sitting under the infamous Moreton Fig Tree on the former Kinchela Boys Home site in October 2016. Photo: Peter Solness

On Saturday, 17 September 2002, fifty men stood with more than two hundred family, friends and community members, on the site of the old Kinchela Boys' Home in New South Wales. They were there to remember the past, which had been hard, violent and cruel, leaving many boys with psychological damage. At this event, generations of boys who were forced to live in Kinchela were honoured; their courage and survival applauded. Some people attended to apologise on behalf of the local government for the gross injustices forced on the Stolen Generations, and these men in particular.

Bill Simon and his three brothers were forcibly taken from their parents while 'waiting for Mum to smear Vegemite on our bread before we dressed for school'. And so began Bill's eight years at Kinchela. Although the boys had a home and parents — they weren't orphans, neglected or abused — they were taken away.

Bill Simon tells about being incarcerated and the effects of the loss of his family in his autobiography, *Back on The Block*: 'I knew nothing of politics, government policies, Protection Boards or the history or the concept of eradicating a whole race. I only felt their effects...Being taken from my parents at such an early age has had its consequences. I often wonder where I'd be had I remained under my father's guidance.'

Unlike many who have struggled with alcoholism and addiction, Bill found salvation through the church and became a pastor in Sydney's Redfern, on The Block, home to many members of the Stolen Generations.

from family and language, many having been told that their families were dead or didn't want them. Some who were institutionalised have grown into adulthood without the love and nurturing most people take for granted. For many, this has affected their ability to run their own households and bring up their own families. It is very painful to listen to parents and children talk about the effect the removals have had on their lives. Some people in Australia claim that the Stolen Generations is a myth, but for us it is a traumatic reality.

The institutions and church missions where most children were placed suppressed their knowledge about their own families, language and culture. In some places discipline was enforced with heartless and brutal punishments.

Rhonda Collard-Spratt's book about her life, *Alice's Daughter* (published by Aboriginal Studies Press) is the story of Rhonda's search for culture and family as she faces violence, racism, foster families, and her father's death in custody — one of the first deaths investigated as part of the Royal Commission into Aboriginal Deaths in Custody.

Aside from some excellent documentaries on this topic, the mainstream release of the film *Rabbit-Proof Fence* was perhaps the first

Left: Rhonda's story was published by Aboriginal Studies Press in 2017.
Right: Aunty Rhonda Collard-Spratt in the sandhills of Miaboolya Beach,
Carnarvon, 2017. Photo courtesy of Aunty Rhonda Collard-Spratt

In 1954, aged three, Rhonda Collard-Spratt was taken from her
Aboriginal family and placed on Carnarvon Native Mission, Western
Australia. Growing up in the white world of chores and aprons,
religious teachings and cruel beatings, Rhonda drew strength and
healing from her mission brothers and sisters, her art, music and
poetry, and her unbreakable bond with the Dreaming.

time that large numbers of non-Indigenous Australians learned of the
immense pain and hardship caused by the removal policy. The film
was based on a book by Doris Pilkington Garimara, who, upon being
reunited with her mother after decades of separation, learned of her
mother and aunts' journey following their removal as children from a
desert community. There are many other examples of child removal
and institutionalisation. Sister Kate's Home, established in Perth in
1930, received many lighter-skinned children taken from their families

by government officials. Much of the pain continues long after we have been reunited with our families as a result of the length of separation. Link-Up is one of several organisations that provide support to people still searching for their families (see Link-up organisations, p. 28).

The Apology

On 13 February 2008, former Prime Minister Kevin Rudd offered an apology to members of the Stolen Generations, which was supported almost unanimously in the House of Representatives. It is known today as simply the Apology.

It was an important day for the nation and seemed to release a tide of goodwill and a commitment to right past wrongs and overcome the social disadvantage of Indigenous Australians, while involving communities in closing the gap (see Closing the gap, p. 64).

Prime Minister Kevin Rudd with women wearing 'Thanks' t-shirts in response to the Apology, 13 February 2008. Photo: Wayne Quilliam

PASTORALISM

Many Aboriginal people across Australia maintained contact with their country by living on pastoral leases, government reserves and Christian missions. We were allowed to do so because we provided an accessible workforce for pastoralists, one they didn't have to pay. The men who lived on the stations worked as seasonal drovers and labourers, while the women were employed throughout the year as domestics, with some women also working with stock on horseback. All were at risk of sexual and physical abuse from non-Indigenous stock workers.

Pastoralists were responsible for the distribution of government-issued rations to those of us who were too old to work. However, in reality they dispensed rations as they chose, sometimes withholding them as a method of discipline. This had a devastating effect on the health of those of us with limited access to bush tucker. The economy of pastoral Australia was sustained by our slave labour, though pastoralists justified not paying Aboriginal workers a cash wage on the basis of poor returns and our supposed unreliability.

In our demands for a fair wage we refused to undertake some tasks, and on occasions, we went on strike. Our initial demands for a fair wage and better treatment of our women later translated into a demand for land (see Strikes and protests, p. 147).

With help from the North Australia Workers Union, the Northern Territory Cattle Station Industry Award Case was held and in 1966 a decision was made that granted equal wages to Aboriginal people. Although long overdue, the equal wages award and its poor implementation in 1968 had devastating consequences. Pastoralists refused to employ us and we were thrown off our Country. In the subsequent exodus into towns, we faced the loss of access to traditional foods and lands, the loss of our skills as well as our self-esteem. Many of us ended up living in fringe settlements with no running water, electricity or housing. Some people had just what they could build out of scraps. We

Wirliyajarrayi

Stockmen in Willowra, Northern Territory, c. 1960. Photo: AIATSIS, Sarah Hale Collection HERD.R01.DF-D00008784/87

Former AIATSIS CEO, Russell Taylor with Jimmy Wavehill at the 2016 Freedom Festival, celebrating the 50th Anniversary of the Wave Hill walk-off. Jimmy had been among the Gurindji people who walked to Wattie Creek with Vincent Lingiari. Photo: Bryce Gray/AIATSIS

faced malnutrition, sickness and abject poverty. Decades later many communities are still recovering.

Missionaries and other humanitarians who actively supported our rights to justice were sometimes removed from their positions, often following strident media campaigns against them. For example, the Reverend Gribble was severely criticised in the nineteenth century by the Western Australian press, pastoralists and politicians, when he tried to intervene on behalf of Aboriginal people cruelly treated by non-Indigenous colonists.

Other well-meaning clergymen and colonial settlers, anxious to uphold decent civil values in our treatment, were ridiculed, silenced or censured, and in time most missions were broken up so that

Archie Roach plays at #Apology10, the 10th Anniversary of the Apology to the Stolen Generations in Canberra, 2018. Courtesy: AIATSIS and Healing Foundation. Photographer: Andrew Turner

surrounding pastoralists could have access to their land. The Buntingdale Mission, established at Birregurra in Victoria in 1839, had been harassed for years by pastoralists accusing it of incompetence and the waste of public money. Several of those leading the complaint, like the grazier William Roadknight, acquired the lands when the missions were abandoned in response to this campaign of public criticism.

Some pastoralists with designs on the land also maligned the Protectors as lazy and ineffectual do-gooders. In time most Protectorate lands were taken over by governments for use by pastoralists and farmers. Land from some mission stations was offered to returned non-Indigenous soldiers, called 'soldier settlers', after the First and Second World Wars.

Under the various Land Rights Acts across the country, beginning with the *Aboriginal Land Trust Act 1966* (SA) and the better known *Aboriginal Land Rights (Northern Territory) Act 1976* (Cth), many of us who remained on the 'mish' — as government reserves and missions were called in some parts of the country — were finally granted ownership of the land. In Victoria, mission stations such as Lake Tyers and Lake Condah are now under our control. Similar things happened at Point McLeay in South Australia and other former reserves in New South Wales, but not Western Australia where the land was not transferred.

ASSIMILIATION

In 1939, John McEwen, then Commonwealth Minister for the Interior, announced a 'New Deal'. This was the first announcement of assimilation as a Commonwealth Government policy and it was formal recognition that we were not dying out as a people, as had been the long-held belief under the Protection Acts. The purpose of assimilation is to absorb a minority group into the dominant cultural group with the ultimate aim of destroying the former. Australia's colonial administrators did not believe there was any benefit in integrating any aspect of Aboriginal culture into the new Australian society, and policies were framed with the object of absorbing into the mainstream society those who were seen to be capable of becoming 'civilised'. Aboriginal people were classified based on 'their degree of Aboriginal blood'; known as blood quantum. People who were considered to be 'full-bloods' were deemed unable to be 'civilised' and were segregated and removed to reserves. People judged to be of 'mixed blood' (a classification that was further defined in racial and racist terms: 'half-caste', 'quadroon', 'octoroon', etc) were considered able to be absorbed into white society. The aim of assimilation was to eradicate Aboriginal identities and 'breed out the Aboriginal race'. Up until the late 1950s states regularly legislated all forms of inclusion and exclusion by reference to degrees of Aboriginal blood.

Assimilation policies required Aboriginal people to give up their culture, kin and history, in order to be seen as 'white'. By achieving this to the satisfaction of the authorities, they would be issued with an

THE LITTLE RED YELLOW BLACK BOOK

exemption certificate and allowed to live as a 'white person', without the heavy restrictions placed on Indigenous Australians, though they still faced the same segregationist and discriminatory practices such as needing approval to marry. One of the most insidious assimilation policies was the taking of children (particularly those of mixed descent) from their families to be raised by white people (see Stolen Generations, p. 126). The enduring and devastating effect of assimilation policies continues to this day. However, despite attempts to eradicate our cultures, identities and communities, we have survived and remain strong.

In New South Wales, assimilation was introduced in 1940 when the Aborigines Welfare Board replaced the old Aborigines Protection Board. It was not until after the Second World War that the other states began to respond to demands for a policy change. For example, the Commonwealth paid child endowment and the old age pension to those of us who met the eligibility criteria, but the states would not. It is arguable, however, how much of those funds actually made it to the intended recipients (see Stolen wages, p. 138).

In 1951, Paul Hasluck was appointed as Commonwealth Minister for Territories. He introduced a new policy of assimilation, elements of which were adopted by the states, although Victoria and Tasmania claimed to have no real 'Aboriginal problem'. The policy of assimilation stated that: '[All] Aborigines shall attain the same manner of living as other Australians, enjoying the same rights and privileges, accepting the same responsibilities, observing the same customs and being influenced by the same beliefs, hopes and loyalties of other Australians.'

By the mid-1960s, opposition to assimilation was strengthening and new policies aimed more at integration were being introduced. The Whitlam government cast aside assimilation as Commonwealth Government policy in December 1972. Instead, a new policy, self-determination, was introduced. This completed the shift in policy development from protection to assimilation to self-determination.

Exemption certificates

After the 1940s, the various state governments brought in exemption certificates for Aboriginal people of mixed decent, which meant we would be exempt from the Aboriginal Protection Acts. With an exemption certificate we could vote, move around as we pleased and take any job. The catch was that to get the exemption, we had to give up our traditional lives and stay far away from other Aboriginal people. People who received the certificate were no longer considered to be Aboriginal and they were not allowed to visit their own families, nor socialise with other Indigenous Australians, under threat of gaol. Many of us came to call them 'dog tags' or 'dog certificates'.

New South Wales Government Certificate of Exemption. Photo: AIATSIS collection Brown C01.BW-N0173603

STOLEN WAGES

From the late 1800s and through much of the twentieth century, governments controlled most aspects of our lives and this included our wages, pensions and endowments. Often we received none of our wage, or only a portion of what was due to us, with the remainder kept in various government trust funds. Much of that money was mismanaged or diverted to other government programs, a fact pointed out to various governments at the time, but ignored. Our families were never shown what money was being held and what was owed them. This practice is now called 'stolen wages'. In mid-2006, the Commonwealth Parliament set up a Senate inquiry into stolen wages, which provided a report and recommendations. To date, no action has been taken on the report, though some states have set up compensation schemes, most of which offer very little and are considered unfair. Various class action suits have been brought against the government. In 2016, Hans Pearson, then 77, became the lead claimant in a class action suit involving around 3,000 Aboriginal people, against the Queensland Government. Hans is suing to recover wages he claims were stolen from him more than half a century ago.

NORTHERN TERRITORY EMERGENCY RESPONSE

In August 2006, the Northern Territory government commissioned research into allegations of serious child sexual abuse in Aboriginal communities. *The little children are sacred* report was released in June 2007. Less than a fortnight later the Howard government staged the Northern Territory Emergency Response (NTER). Now commonly called 'the Intervention', the legislation responded to few of the report's ninety-seven recommendations.

Wide-ranging changes occurred, facilitated by police and the army. In the 'prescribed areas', where Aboriginal people are in the majority, alcohol and pornographic material was banned, there was an increased police presence, children were provided with health checks and efforts made to enforce school attendance. The Commonwealth acquired five-year leases over declared Aboriginal land, 'community living areas' and town camps. Customary law was excluded as a factor in sentencing and bail decisions, income management was applied to residents in prescribed and other declared areas, a review of income-management decisions was denied and changes to permits allowed greater access to Aboriginal land by non-Aboriginal people.

More than 600,000 square kilometres of country was affected as were the lives of approximately 45,500 Aboriginal people.

Effectively, the legislation suspended the operation of the Racial Discrimination Act (RDA), as acts undertaken as part of the NTER were to be 'special measures'. Rather than being positive measures benefitting Aboriginal people, the 'special measures' restricted the rights of some or all members of the affected communities.

The Gillard government published an independent review in October 2008. The government then consulted with Aboriginal people (though some were critical of that process) and on 1 July 2010 the legislated changes came into effect.

These changes included formally lifting the suspension of the RDA. However, it did not end all intervention measures that were racially targeted and it fails to meet the principles of the UN Declaration on the Rights of Indigenous Peoples (supported by Australia in April 2009) through the right to free, prior and informed consent.

The Intervention has received bi-partisan support but there have been strong criticisms from the Social Justice Commissioner (2008) and the UN Special Rapporteur, James Anaya (2009). The NTER and the subsequent Stronger Futures legislation which passed the Senate in June 2012 and extends the Intervention for years, provoked strong community reactions, although there are a diversity of views among communities about the success and fairness of measures. It's been over ten years since the NTER was established and all studies point to it as a failure in closing the gap, yet despite wide-spread protests the Intervention was extended until 2022.

Recruit Michaelyn Waia after graduating from the Defence Indigenous
Development Program (DIDP) Course 7 at HMAS Cairns, Queensland.
© Commonwealth of Australia, Department of Defence

OUR
LEADERSHIP
AND ACTIVISM

Cultural resistance is arguably one of the most important forms of survival. Aboriginal and Torres Strait Islander peoples have fought to retain our languages and ways of life, and our many cultures are proudly seen as the longest ongoing living cultures in the world. Our warriors include not only those who served with honour and pride in Australia's military, but our ancestral warriors who fought against colonial invasion and occupation over many years. Today our modern-day warriors continue the fight to maintain our culture, battle against racism and work in defence of our sovereignty and rights to self-determination.

RESISTANCE

Early warriors and leaders

Jandamarra

In the late 1800s, in the central Kimberley region of Western Australia, Jandamarra, a Bunuba man, used every ounce of his knowledge of Country to hold off the encroachment of pastoralists on his land. He was taught by his uncle, Ellemarra, in the rituals of Bunuba manhood and the two shared an exceptionally close bond. On 31 October 1894, a large group of Bunuba elders, including Jandamarra's uncle, had been captured after repeated reprisals against the colonialists. Jandamarra shot station owner Bill Richardson to free them and the group became outlaws on their own country. Jandamarra began a guerrilla war from hideouts in the caves and surrounding ranges of Windjana Gorge and Tunnel Creek, targeting encroachers on Bunuba land. In desperation the police hired an Aboriginal tracker from the Pilbara to hunt him down. Jandamarra was tracked to a cave system at Tunnel Creek and after an exchange of fire he was shot and killed. In a final act of mockery against Jandamarra, the Lennard River police beheaded his corpse as a trophy and sent it to Britain as a scientific specimen.

Pemulwuy

The warrior Pemulwuy of the Bidjigal nation, located in today's western Sydney, speared a frontier man in 1790 as punishment for killing

Bidjigal people. Governor Phillip retaliated by ordering his staff to kill ten 'natives' and capture two in order to stop further reprisals. Fifty soldiers and two surgeons were sent into the bush, but not a single Aboriginal person was captured. The Eora and Bidjigal people, led by Pemulwuy, then undertook a campaign of resistance against the British colonisers in a series of attacks during the late 1700s. In 1801, Governor King issued an order that Aboriginal people near Parramatta, Georges River and Prospect could be shot on sight, and in November a proclamation outlawed Pemulwuy and offered a reward for his death or capture. In June 1802 Pemulwuy was shot and killed in an ambush. Many consider Pelmuwuy as the first Australian patriot — the first Australian to defend this country against a foreign invader.

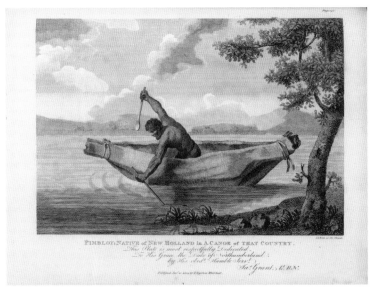

PIMBLOY: NATIVE of NEW HOLLAND in A CANOE of THAT COUNTRY.

This engraving by James Grant of 'Pimbloy' is believed to be the only known depiction of Pemulwuy. Illustration courtesy of the National Library of Australia, from Grant's 'The narrative of a voyage of discovery, performed in His Majesty's vessel the Lady Nelson, of sixty tons burthen, with sliding keels, in the years 1800, 1801 and 1802, to New South Wales, 1803'. NLA.CAT-VN2312357

Tarenorerer

Tarenorerer (or Walyer) was born in Tasmania around 1800. It is believed that Tarenorerer was sold to white sealers on the Bass Strait Islands in her teens after being abducted by Aboriginal people of the Port Sorell region. She quickly learnt to speak English fluently, and also learnt how to shoot a gun during her time with the sealers.

In 1828 she escaped from the sealers and returned to her Country, where she gathered men and women from different groups to initiate warfare against the invaders. She personally trained her warriors in the use of firearms and in effective battle tactics against the slow to load guns of her enemies, and introduced guerrilla warfare strategies of killing livestock. She's believed to have said 'she liked a *luta tawin* (white man) as she did a black snake'.

Walyer by Julie Dowling, 2006. Licensed by VISCOPY Australia

Abducted again by sealers, she was taken to Bird Island. She hid her identity and was known to the sealers only as 'Mary Anne'. In 1830 she was taken to Swan Island after it was believed she was plotting to murder one of the sealers, and her true identity was soon revealed. She was kept in isolation for fear that she would incite a revolt on the island. She became ill and died of influenza on 5 June 1831.

Windradyne

Windradyne, a Wiradjuri warrior, was a key resistance figure in the Bathurst War in 1824. When Governor Brisbane came to power the pace of settlement greatly increased west of the Blue Mountains, increasing competition on traditional food sources. Windradyne began leading attacks on small farming outposts using guerrilla warfare techniques. In December 1823 he was blamed for the death of two stockmen and imprisoned.

After he was released, the hostilities continued to escalate with Aboriginal women and children being killed and seven stockmen attacked in the Wyagdon Ranges. The town of Bathurst was finally placed under martial law in 1924 and a reward issued for Windradyne's capture.

Windradyne had been closely associated with George Suttor and his son William Henry, who were strong advocates on behalf of Aboriginal people during and after the period of martial law. Windradyne had been placed at the scene of attacks in Wyagdon in 1829 where it is said that he spared the lives of the Suttor family.

Windradyne managed to avoid capture and was later pardoned by the Governor when he appeared at the annual feast in Parramatta.

Yagan

Yagan (c.1795–1833) was in his early 30s when the area on the western coast of Australia that became Perth was colonised by the British in 1829. He befriended many of the early settlers and was well-known in the Perth district. The *Perth Gazette* published stories about him and George Fletcher Moore, a prominent early settler, described encounters with Yagan in his diaries.

After a number of clashes with settlers, over food and other resources, Yagan was declared an outlaw and forced to go into hiding. Tragically, on 11 July 1833, Yagan's friend William Keates shot and killed Yagan for a £30 reward.

After his death Yagan's body was decapitated, preserved and taken to England as a scientific curio. Yagan is well-known to both Indigenous and non-Indigenous people and remains a symbolic figure in contemporary Noongar history. In the 1950s Noonger man Ken Colbung began a search for Yagan's remains, they were found in an unmarked grave in Liverpool and, after a long campaign, repatriated to Australia and Noongar land in 1997.

William Barak Bridge, Melbourne. Photo: Meyer Eidelsen

Many landmarks in our cities are named after some of our great leaders and warriors. For example, if you're in Melbourne it's likely that you've driven over the William Barak Bridge. William Barak, *Ngurungaeta*, was the clan leader of the Wurundjeri. As a boy, he was present at the signing of John Batman's treaty. An outstanding leader in the struggle for Aboriginal rights and justice, he guided his people with courage and wisdom through extraordinary times.

ACTIVISM

Strikes and protests

In January 1936, the Torres Strait Islanders working on the company boats fishing in the Strait went on strike, protesting against the constraints they experienced under the *Aboriginal Protection Act*. Non-violent, organised secretly and using Islander networks to transmit messages, the strike led to the *Torres Strait Islanders Act 1939*. This resulted in Torres Strait Islanders being distinguished in law from Aboriginal people legislatively, although the government still retained enormous control over their lives. The Queensland Government allowed the creation of an inter-island organisation, known since 1984 as the Island Coordinating Council.

One of the earliest protests by Aboriginal or Torres Strait Islander workers for fairer working conditions was the Torres Strait Maritime Strike. In January 1936 approximately 70 per cent of the Torres Strait Islander workforce, mostly those who worked on pearling boats, went on strike.

Men on pearling boats, Thursday Island, Torres Strait, c. 1930–40s. Photo: AIATSIS Collection CANE.F01.BW-N0010221

Lasting up to nine months on some islands, the strike brought about significant changes in working conditions and the establishment of the Island Advisory Council, which gave Torres Strait Islanders significant autonomy in managing their own affairs.

From 1946–49, in a sign of things to come, Aboriginal station workers throughout the Pilbara region of Western Australia went on strike, the longest in Australia's history. Eight hundred people walked off about twenty stations, paralysing the local sheep industry. People lived in temporary camps and collected pearl shell, and some set up their own mining operations. Eventually there was some improvement in wages and conditions but nothing long-lasting.

Workers strikes were always about more than just fairer working conditions and equal wages.

Gurindji strikers at Wattie Creek, Northern Territory, next to the sign that asserted their claim over their lands, 1967. Photo: Brian Manning

In 1966, 170 Gurindji people walked off Lord Vestey's Wave Hill station in the Northern Territory and gathered at a place called Wattie Creek, which was known to Gurindji as Dagaragu. Originally understood as a strike against poor working conditions, the walk-off was primarily a demand for Gurindji autonomy and the return of traditional lands.

Although it was not the first demand for Aboriginal land rights, it was the first to attract significant public support both in Australia and internationally. The walk-off had strong support from the Australian Workers' Union and was a crucial moment in the step towards the *Aboriginal Land Rights (Northern Territory) Act 1976* (Cth).

Today, on Gurindji Freedom Day, the Gurindji celebrate the achievement of those who fought for their land rights.

Organisational activism

Well-known New South Wales activist, Fred Maynard, founded the Australian Aboriginal Progressive Association (AAPA) in 1924. The AAPA organised street rallies, held well-publicised regional and metropolitan meetings, and showed great skill in using newspaper coverage, letter-writing campaigns and petitions to lobby for our cause. It collaborated with the international black rights movement through Maynard's connections with Marcus Garvey, first president of the Universal Negro Improvement Association in the USA. Sadly, the AAPA's central demands still strike a chord today: recognition of Aboriginal rights to land, stopping Aboriginal children being stolen from their families, and defending a distinct Aboriginal cultural identity.

Another strand in the movements towards land rights was the establishment in 1958 of the first national organisation for Indigenous Australians, the Federal Council for the Advancement of Aborigines in 1958. Later known as FCAATSI, the organisation included supportive non-Indigenous people in its early years, and took a leading role in the success of the 1967 Referendum. After the referendum win FCAATSI became an all-Indigenous Australian body.

Faith Bandler, Turramurra, New South Wales, ca. 1975, © Bruce Howard.

In 1963, Faith Bandler became the New South Wales state secretary of the Federal Council for Aboriginal Advancement representing the interests of Aboriginal people from New South Wales. In 1967, after the federal government had agreed to hold a referendum on the 'Aboriginal question', Bandler was appointed New South Wales campaign director, a position she fulfilled with energy, skill and enthusiasm.

The formation of FCAATSI coincided with a global movement to challenge racism in Europe, Africa and the United States. In Australia students from The University of Sydney burned the American flag to protest against racial segregation in the United States and were criticised in the press for ignoring similar conditions in Australia.

While other Australians took part in the 150th anniversary celebrations in 1938 of the First Fleet landing at Botany Bay, some of us took part in a protest. William Cooper, the founder of the Australian Aborigines' League, was deeply disappointed at the lack of progress in his attempts to encourage the Commonwealth Government to make reforms in Aboriginal administration. He persuaded John Patten and William Ferguson, leaders of the Aborigines Progressive Association (APA), to organise a protest. On 26 January 1938, Aboriginal people observed the first 'Day of Mourning'. About 100 Aboriginal people, and four non-Aboriginal people, attended a conference on the day.

A later delegation presented then Prime Minister Joseph Lyons with a proposed national policy for Aboriginal people that had been drawn up and signed off at the conference. The policy was rejected on the pretext that the Commonwealth had limited constitutional responsibility for Aboriginal affairs. Patten wrote the manifesto, 'Aborigines Claim Citizenship Rights!' and we now remember 26 January as 'Invasion Day' or 'Survival Day'.

The 1967 Referendum

The year 1967 saw the culmination of a valiant campaign fought by FCAATSI and others to encourage the Australian people to accept a referendum to change the Constitution. Many people mistakenly believe that the 1967 Referendum gave us the right to vote, but this was not the case. The change would allow Aboriginal people to be included in the census and would enable the Commonwealth to make laws for Aboriginal and Torres Strait Islander people. In the drafting of the Australian Constitution of 1901, the colonies had said they wanted to retain their powers to make laws concerning Aboriginal people within

Community members protesting that people in the Northern Territory were not entitled to vote in the 1967 Referendum. Photo: AIATSIS collection DOWNING.J01. CS-000055722

their territory, including those laws that discriminated against them. The Constitution therefore specifically prohibited the Commonwealth Government from making laws in relation to Aboriginal people. It was hoped that the referendum would allow the Commonwealth Government to overturn discriminatory laws and better protect Aboriginal and Torres Strait Islander people.

With its 90.77 per cent 'Yes' vote, the referendum was passed in all six states. It remains one of the most successful national campaigns in our history. However, limited positive changes were made to the lives of Aboriginal and Torres Strait Islander people as a result of the 1967 Referendum. Today, a close examination of the campaign and the changes to the Constitution reveal that there were limits to what might have been expected.

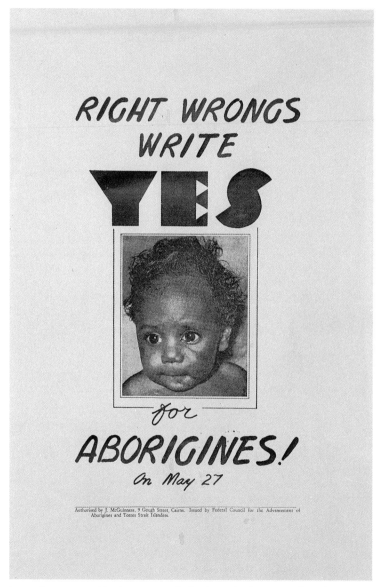

Image from a pamphlet in support of a 'Yes' vote in the 1967 Referendum.
Photo: AIATSIS collection DAA.003.BW-N04528_13A

DID YOU KNOW?

The Australian Constitution said that 'in reckoning the numbers of people of the Commonwealth, or of a State or other part of the Commonwealth, [A]boriginal natives shall not be counted' (Section 127 xxvi). A few of us could vote at state level before Federation in 1901, Queensland and Western Australia being the only states that expressly forbade Indigenous Australians from voting. The *Commonwealth Electoral Act 1918* allowed only those few who were already allowed to vote to keep that right and even gave them the right to vote at a federal level, but the rest of us were no longer allowed to do either. It wasn't until 1962, when the electoral act was amended, that we were given the right to register and vote, but voting was not compulsory. Full voting rights were not granted federally until Aboriginal and Torres Strait Islander people were required to register on the electoral roll in 1984.

Yirrkala Bark Petition

In 1963, the Yolngu people of Yirrkala in north-east Arnhem Land presented a bark petition to the Commonwealth Parliament. It was their response to the threat to their country posed by bauxite mining. These documents are the first traditional documents recognised by the Commonwealth Parliament. They combined traditional bark painting with text typed on paper. The painted designs proclaim Yolngu Law, revealing the people's traditional relationship to the land. The text is in English and Gumatj languages. Although the Yolngu didn't achieve the constitutional change they wanted, they helped pave the way for the recognition of Aboriginal and Torres Strait Islander rights in Australian law. The following court case, known as the Gove land rights case in 1971, ended with the court rejecting the Rirratjingu clan's claim because their

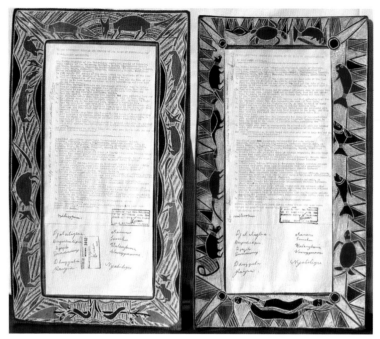

Left: Yirrkala artists, Dhuwa moiety, Yirrkala Bark Petition 14.8.1963 46.9 x 21 cm,
Right: Yirrkala artists, Yirritja moiety, Yirrkala Bark Petition 28.8.1963 46.9 x 21 cm,
natural ochres on bark, ink on paper, House of Representatives, Canberra

relationship to the land didn't fit the European concept of 'property',
despite the court acknowledging that Aboriginal people had a 'subtle
and elaborate system' of 'social rules and customs' that 'provided a
stable order of society'. The judge was bound by early decisions that had
said that regardless of the facts, as a matter of British law, Aboriginal
people had no recognisable system of law.

Freedom Rides

In 1965, Charles Perkins, one of the first Aboriginal university graduates,
led a group of our people and supporters on a 'Freedom Ride' — a
bus tour of outback New South Wales. The action was based on the
US Freedom Rides and sought to highlight blatant racism. At that time,

In February 1965 the Student Action for Aborigines Organisation at The University of Sydney set off on the Freedom Ride. Led by Charles Perkins, approximately 35 students, travelling by bus, embarked on a mission to see for themselves how segregated life in Australia was. Photograph reproduced with permission of Wendy Watson-Ekstein (née Golding) and supplied by Ann Curthoys

we were barred from using public venues, including swimming pools, in many Australian country communities. The Freedom Riders caused enormous controversy across the nation as Australians were shown the true nature of race relations.

The Tent Embassy

Tired of having legitimate claims denied, on Australia Day 1972 four Aboriginal men (Michael Anderson, Billy Craigie, Tony Coorey and Bertie Williams) erected a tent on the lawns of old Parliament House in Canberra. Joined by other Aboriginal activists they told police that the tent was an Aboriginal embassy and they would stay until the government granted land rights. The embassy's petition, a five-point plan, addressed Aboriginal ownership of existing reserves and settlements (including rights to mineral deposits), ownership of land in the capital

Chicka Dixon (left) and Paul Coe (right) at the Aboriginal Tent Embassy in front of Parliament House. Photo: AIATSIS collection JACKOMOS.A04.BW-N03770_23a

cities (including mineral rights), preservation of all sacred sites in all parts of the continent, six million dollars in compensation, and full rights of statehood for the Northern Territory.

Despite various attempts to dismantle it using police force, local ordinances, planning guidelines and direct negotiation (even attempts to burn it down), the Embassy remains to this day on the lawns of old Parliament House. It has been the centre of protest and the starting point for marches on Parliament demanding sovereignty and a treaty. Authorities have found it difficult to counter the Tent Embassy's mixture of persistent grass-roots politics and symbolism, with some Aboriginal people now talking about the site's sacredness. Called an embassy because it represents a displaced nation, in 1995 it was listed on the Australian Heritage Council's national estate.

The Aboriginal Tent embassy, like the Freedom Rides, became a powerful symbol of resistance and cultural revival. It remains as a

The Aboriginal Tent Embassy in Canberra, c. 1980. Photo: AIATSIS Collection
DAA.003.BW-N04528_24A

thorn in the side of the Australian conscience, reminding Australians that the work of forging a treaty has hardly begun. The year 2012 marked the 40th anniversary of the Tent Embassy, and serves as a reminder that the claims to land rights and a treaty still have not been met.

SOVEREIGNTY

The *Mabo case* and the *Native Title Act*

In 1982 Edward Koiki Mabo, along with fellow Mer Islanders, Reverend David Passi, Celuia Mapoo Salee and James Rice, launched a case in the High Court of Australia. In an historic judgment ten years later, the Court held that Meriam people possess rights to their traditional lands and that these rights should be recognised and protected by Australian law.

The Mabo decision challenged the existing Australian legal system: by correcting the assumptions firstly that Aboriginal and Torres Strait Islander peoples had no concept of land ownership before the arrival of British colonisers in 1788 (the Australian continent was considered to be *terra nullius*, or 'no one's land', meaning land over which no previous sovereignty has been exercised) and secondly that sovereignty delivered complete ownership of all land in the new colony to the Crown and abolished any of our pre-existing rights. Finally, it could no longer be argued that Australia was a land without law before the arrival of the colonisers, and it forced non-Indigenous Australians to confront the injustices of the colonising system.

The Mer Islanders' action followed the earlier unsuccessful legal action taken in the 1971 Gove land rights case in the Northern Territory

Djuki Mala performing at the Uluru Handback Anniversary concert, 2015. The 'Handover' (as it was then called) of Uluru in 1985 was a symbolic highpoint for land rights. The land had been alienated from the *Aboriginal Land Rights (Northern Territory) Act 1976* by the declaration of the Uluru and Kata Tjuta (Ayers Rock and Mt Olga) National Park in 1977. In the late 1970s Traditional Owners, the Pitjantjatjara Council and the Central Land Council, lobbied the government and in 1985 the federal government signed over the title deeds to Uluru. Five minutes later the Traditional Owners signed an agreement leasing the park back to the Australian Parks and Wildlife Service for 99 years. Photo: AIATSIS/John Paul Janke

Supreme Court; *Milirrpum v Nabalco Pty Ltd* (1971). In the *Milirrpum* case, the plaintiffs: Milirrpum, Munggurrawuy and Daymbalipu were members respectively of the Rirratjingu, Gumatj and Djapu clans of the Yolngu peoples. The plaintiffs claimed that they held existing rights under their customs that needed to be respected. The Court rejected this argument and found that, even though the Yirrkala had a 'subtle and elaborate' system of law, Indigenous Australian relationships to land were fundamentally religious. The Court found that there was no doctrine of Aboriginal or native title in Australian law. This was later overturned by the *Mabo* decision in the High Court of Australia in 1992.

The *Mabo* decision recognised the historical and lived connections of our many peoples to land and waters, and the rights and interests that flow from these relationships as part of the doctrine of native title that now forms part of the Australian legal system. After much negotiation and parliamentary debate, the Commonwealth Government passed a new law dealing with land rights called the *Native Title Act 1993* (Cth). A process was developed to work out whether native title exists in particular areas, and how future activity over lands can go ahead when it has an impact on native title. The law also made provisions for us to be compensated where our native title is reduced or wiped out.

Since the *Mabo* case, decisions made by judges in native title cases and amendments to the law have considerably reduced the potential of the native title law to recognise the rights of all Indigenous Australians. This has led Indigenous Australian groups and governments to look to alternative ways of resolving the outstanding issues of land justice. Other methods such as reaching agreements in the form of Indigenous Land Use Agreements or ILUAs, have emerged as a strong basis for developing ongoing relationships with government and industry. It is important to remember that the developing common law of native title is constantly changing: sometimes for the benefit and at other times for the detriment of our rights.

Professor Mick Dodson is a member of the Yawuru peoples — the Traditional Owners of land and waters in the Broome area of the southern Kimberley region of Western Australia. He was Australia's first Aboriginal and Torres Strait Islander Social Justice Commissioner with the Human Rights Commission. Professor Dodson spent a quarter of a century

Professor Mick Dodson. Photo: AIATSIS

on the AIATSIS Council, seventeen years as its Chairperson and was the Director of the National Centre for Indigenous Studies at the ANU. He has been and is a prominent advocate on land rights and other issues affecting Aboriginal and Torres Strait Islander peoples, as well as a vigorous advocate of the rights and interests of indigenous peoples around the world.

By June 2017, there were 385 registered determinations of native title covering a total area of approximately 2,626,924 sq. km or 34.2 per cent of the land mass of Australia and approximately 100,217 sq. km of sea (below the low-water mark). There are 1174 ILUAs on the Register of Indigenous Land Use Agreements. Native title remains a form of 'justice in transition' that needs careful review to make it a fairer, faster and more workable system for all. Unfortunately, the process can pitch one set of claimants against another, creating or intensifying divisions within our communities. The struggle for our rights to our land and waters has been fought over decades. These legal challenges have taken their toll on the health of our leaders and our non-Indigenous advisers and supporters. There are many cases still to be heard and many elders will not see the day their lands and waters are returned. In his 2017 address to the ceremonial sitting of the Federal Court of Australia, marking its 40th anniversary, Professor Mick Dodson said that native title claims need to be resolved through good faith negotiations and settlements.

With recognition, however, we as native title holders enjoy much greater protection of our rights and interests in our traditional country, which both state and federal governments must respect. For us, it is not merely a form of title but a fundamental recognition of our unique identity as the first peoples of Australia.

Compensation for loss or impairment of native title is available according to our constitutional rights concerning the compulsory acquisition of property under the Commonwealth Constitution

Gunggandji-Mandingalbay Yidinji Peoples celebrate the joint determination in 2011 at the Cairns Court House.

(s51 xxxi of the Constitution). The first significant native title case setting out the principles for compensation for loss or impairment of our native title rights was decided in 2016. The native title determinations of the Ngaliwurru and Nungali peoples were made in 1999 and 2000 over lands and waters in the township of Timber Creek, 400 km south of Darwin. The Ngaliwurru and Nungali peoples application for compensation for loss of native title made pursuant to section 61 of the *Native Title Act 1993* (Cth) was decided by Justice Mansfield on 24 August 2016 in *Griffiths v Northern Territory (No. 3)* [2016] FCA 900 (Griffiths #3).

DID YOU KNOW?

Ensuring that Aboriginal and Torres Strait Islander individuals enjoy the human rights and freedoms we all hold, equally and without discrimination, is the basis of self-determination. It includes social and cultural rights but also such things as political participation, education, employment rights and economic rights. We as Aboriginal and Torres Strait Islander peoples exercise self-determination every day through simple acts of maintaining our cultural traditions, speaking language, living and getting back on Country, taking young people fishing and hunting, and establishing livelihoods that continue to connect us to our social and cultural practices.

Peak bodies

Over the years a number of regional and national peak bodies have emerged to represent the interests of, and provide support to, particular Aboriginal groups or community organisations. Other peak bodies have been initiated by governments. Some of the national peak bodies include: the Australian Indigenous Doctors' Association; the National Native Title Council; the Stolen Generations Alliance; the First Peoples Disability Network; and the National Family Violence Prevention Legal Services.

Aboriginal and Torres Strait Islander Commission

In 1987, the federal government established the Aboriginal and Torres Strait Islander Commission (ATSIC). The new Commission combined some existing government organisations and took on the functions of the federal departments of Aboriginal Affairs, the Aboriginal Development Commission and Aboriginal Hostels. Attempts by earlier governments to involve us included the national Aboriginal Conference and, before that, the national Aboriginal Consultative Committee, which the government of the time found to be assertive and confrontational. ATSIC later took over the representative functions of the national Aboriginal Conference.

All three organisations were created by governments, with little input from our communities. The organisations were constrained by government legislation, parts of which were created for political purposes rather than to achieve things for our people. ATSIC was meant to represent different regions through elections, but it was also responsible for delivering programs and funding that was generally inadequate for the organisation's needs. The ATSIC commissioners found themselves unsure of their roles, with staff reporting to the ATSIC Board as well as the Minister. The disbanding of ATSIC in March 2004 was done without proper consultation with Aboriginal leaders, and despite the findings of the government's own review of ATSIC. Even if flawed, ATSIC was blamed for failures that fell outside of its responsibilities and obligations.

After the Labor electoral win in November 2007, the new Prime Minister, Kevin Rudd, abolished the National Indigenous Council created by the former federal government, and began consultations to establish a new organisation to represent Aboriginal and Torres Strait Islander people at the federal level, with discussion papers being written and considered. In January 2008, Indigenous Affairs Minister Jenny Macklin scrapped the board.

National Congress of Australia's First Peoples

Created in 2010, the National Congress of Australia's First Peoples gives our people a say on important issues. It provides a national voice for us to be heard by all Australians. It is owned and controlled by its membership and is independent of government.

The National Congress of Australia's First Peoples Executive team 2017: Co-Chair Rod Little, Co-Chair Jackie Huggins and CEO Gary Oliver. Photo: The National Congress of Australia's First Peoples

Inaugural co-Chair, Dr Kerry Arabena, believes that having a national voice is essential. 'Since the abolition of ATSIC, we have not had a national voice which could harness the collective energies and efforts of individuals in communities, service provider organisations and peak bodies,' she says. 'As one of our members commented, "We need to have as much influence as the mining companies do in parliamentary decision-making in Australia".'

After national elections, the board took office on 8 July 2011. The first elected co-Chairs were Les Malezer from the Butchulla/Gubbi Gubbi peoples, and Jody Broun, a Yindjibarndi woman from the Pilbara.

DID YOU KNOW?

Aboriginal Land Councils are regional organisations made up of people elected from the communities who represent and provide a strong voice for their communities. They help people get back on Country; consult with landowners on mining, employment and development; help resolve land disputes; and protect Aboriginal culture and sacred sites. The Kimberley Land Council was formed in 1978 by Kimberley Aboriginal people as a political land rights organisation and it will celebrate its 40th anniversary in 2018. The KLC covers about 423,000 sq. km with an estimated population of 35,000 people. The KLC was set-up for the benefit of all Kimberley Aboriginal people and works with about 25 native title groups to improve their socioeconomic circumstances. The KLC is one of the biggest employers in the Kimberley, employing about 130 staff across the divisions of native title, legal, land and sea management, corporate services; finance and a large ranger network.

National Referendum Council and Constitutional recognition

There are no historical treaties in Australia. In the recent past treaty proposals were focussed on regional settlements and localised policies and funding that support remote areas of limited self-governance. Accommodating the right of self-government within the current constitutional legal arrangements may be more challenging for federal and state governments. Local government, or localised government arrangements, are being pursued, however, the difficulty is where and how to accommodate them within the existing tiers of government in Australia.

In 2012 a panel of experts on the recognition of Aboriginal and Torres Strait Islander peoples in the Constitution gave their report to the

Noel Pearson speaking about Constitutional Recognition at the National Native Title Conference in Townsville, 2017. Photo: AIATSIS

167

Megan Davis, Pat Anderson from the Referendum Council holding the Uluru Statement and Noel Pearson. Photo: Alex Ellinghausen

Commonwealth Joint Select Committee on Constitutional Recognition of Aboriginal and Torres Strait Islander Peoples. The Committee reported back to the Australian Parliament in 2015.

The Aboriginal and Torres Strait Islander Steering Committee of the Referendum Council (a group appointed by the Prime Minister and Opposition Leader in December 2015) said that they would lead and progress the next steps towards a referendum to recognise us in the Constitution from December 2016.

Regional discussions took place over three days with local Traditional Owners and native title companies, leaders from community organisations and other local individuals. The regional dialogues gave their views and this led to the Uluru Convention. Each regional meeting decided on its own delegates to the Uluru Convention.

The Uluru statement represents a major milestone in our reforms as Aboriginal and Torres Strait Islander peoples towards constitutional recognition.

Lisa, Lyndsey and Brooke Fuller, Gold Coast, 2011. Photo courtesy Fuller family photo collection.

The Uluru statement was our way of asserting our sovereignty over lands and waters working alongside the legal idea of the sovereignty of the Crown.

The Uluru statement called for us as first peoples to have a voice, to have a treaty and for a process of truth-telling to take place. The Uluru statement asked for a Makarrata Commission to oversee a national treaty framework and a truth-telling process about Australia's history from our perspectives as Aboriginal and Torres Strait Islander peoples and not just from the perspective of the Europeans who came to our lands.

In asking for a formal process for treaty or agreement making, we as Aboriginal and Torres Strait Islander peoples are asking for our international human right to self-determination, autonomy and self-government and for the ability to express our sovereignty as first peoples.

On 30 June 2017, the Referendum Council reported to the Prime Minister and Opposition Leader. The report was released on 17 July 2017.

On Thursday, 26 October 2017, despite all of the work that had been done on the Uluru statement, the federal government made a decision not to refer the recommendations contained in the Uluru statement to a referendum.

A Treaty?

Behind all these campaigns the notion of a treaty between Indigenous and non-Indigenous Australia still lingers. There has never been a negotiated settlement to transfer lands and sovereignty from Aboriginal and Torres Strait Islander peoples to the British or, now, Australian colonial state. Some say this puts a legal question mark over Australia's sovereignty.

The potential legal or moral legitimacy that such an agreement would bring, however, is sometimes seen as secondary to the symbolic or reconciliatory benefits that would result. In particular, for Indigenous Australians to be formally part of the 'constitutional'

DID YOU KNOW?

It's often said that 'Australia can't make a treaty with itself'. But this is misleading. The term 'treaty' comes from contract law and simply means to 'agree to terms through an offer and acceptance'. Treaties are an internationally accepted form of reaching agreement between Indigenous peoples and states, particularly about issues of land, self-government, and how the relationship between Indigenous governing bodies and the state will be conducted.

make-up of the country would provide a sense of social inclusion that could have a direct impact on the mental well-being of individuals, and change the perception of many non-Indigenous Australians about the nature of a shared history and shared future.

It is often thought that it would be too hard to reach agreement on a single national document, and various models of regional approaches have been investigated. For example, constitutional recognition and protection against racial discrimination is often put forward as an alternative to a national treaty, with a system of locally-based settlements underpinned by a national framework.

At the moment three Australian states — Victoria, South Australia and the Northern Territory — are presently working towards a state-based treaty framework.

Torres Strait Treaty

The Torres Strait Treaty, an agreement signed in 1978 between Australia and Papua New Guinea, defines the boundaries between the two countries and outlines how the sea area may be used. Besides defining the seabed boundary, it allocates rights over fish between the two countries and protects customary rights, including fishing and free movement across the border, in an area called the 'Protected Zone', which covers about two-thirds of the Torres Strait.

Parliamentary representation

Since Federation in 1901, there have been several Indigenous Australian members in the Federal Parliament. Senator Neville Bonner Liberal Senator for the state of Queensland (1971–1983), was the first Indigenous Member of Parliament in 1971. Joanna Lindgren, Liberal Senator for Queensland who served from 2015 to 2016, is the great-niece of Neville Bonner. David Kennedy was the first Indigenous Australian person to be elected to both a state parliament and the Federal Parliament, having served as the Australian Labor Party Member for Bendigo (1969–1972) prior to entering the Victorian Parliament in 1982 as a member of the Legislative Assembly for the Australian Labor Party. However, David Kennedy's Indigeneity was not known when he entered both parliaments, nor did he self-identify as Indigenous Australian at that time. It is for these reasons that Senator Neville Bonner is recorded as the first Indigenous federal parliamentarian.

Mr Ken Wyatt AM MP (2010–present) became the first Indigenous parliamentarian to hold ministerial office as a member of the Cabinet in the Commonwealth Parliament as the Assistant Minister for Health and Aged Care. Linda Burney is the first Indigenous Australian female member of the House of Representatives, elected in 2016 and a representative of the Australian Labor Party and the Federal seat of Barton. She was also the first and only Indigenous member of the New South Wales Parliament, having been elected in 2003 (2003–2016 as the member for Canterbury in the NSW Legislative Assembly). She and Malarndirri McCarthy were the first Indigenous Australian women to be elected to both a state/territory parliament and the Federal Parliament. Senator Nova Peris OAM, was the first female Indigenous Australian senator, serving from 2013 to 2016 as representative of the Australian Labor Party and senator for the Northern Territory.

The Hon. Linda Burney MP, Wiradjuri woman and Member of Parliament. Photo courtesy of Linda Burney

There have been many more First Nations Australians elected to state and territory governments.

While politicians represent all members of their electorate, they bring important experience and expertise to government decisions and policies, especially those which affect Aboriginal and Torres Strait Islander people.

In his inspiring maiden speech to the Australian Parliament in September 2010, Ken Wyatt said:

> Aboriginal and Torres Strait Islander people and the agencies of government need to jettison the old mindsets that embody Indigenous Australians as passive recipients of government programs and services, and to instead truly regard people as equals and allow them to be equal partners in developing their solutions.

More of our people have also served in political life and in the public service, many doing so as a means to help our people, and also to help educate the wider community.

During the 2016 federal election a coalition of Aboriginal and Torres Strait Islander leaders sent a signed statement with a vision for Aboriginal and Torres Strait Islander affairs called the Redfern Statement, to all major political parties, 10 June 2016, Sydney. Photo: SBS

Reconciliation Australia staff member and Bagarrmuguwarra Bama man, Thaarramali Pearson, attended the National Indigenous Youth Parliament (NIYP) held in Canberra in May 2017. The NIYP brought together fifty future Indigenous leaders from around Australia to talk about issues affecting their communities. Photo: AIATSIS

Making decisions for our communities

Reconciliation Australia is an organisation which recognises that the main ingredient in overturning disadvantage in our communities is to make good decisions for and within those communities. Reconciliation Australia emphasises that good decision making only comes about when we as Indigenous peoples have real power to make decisions about policies affecting our own communities. A crucial factor in the success of any program to improve our health, education and employ-ment is to support and encourage our communities to manage our own services. To that end, Reconciliation Australia has worked with BHB Billiton and other transnational corporations and the federal govern-ment to promote good governance skills and research.

Doctors, nurses and teachers have recommended for decades that the health and education services, particularly in remote communities, should be managed under the authority of those local communities. Local land councils and cooperatives have been delivering such services in some locations for decades. Care for pregnant women, after-school programs, kindergartens, elderly citizen homes, drug and alcohol rehabilitation, sports organisations, art and culture centres, housing cooperatives and archaeological services are just some of the success stories springing from community-controlled administration. Allowing our elders and communities to manage solutions, with access to sufficient staff and funds, is crucial for these programs to run successfully and efficiently.

Where our communities have been able to take an active and equal role in negotiating participation in mining, tourism, and heritage enterprises, the results have usually been advantageous for us.

In the Torres Strait, there has been some form of locally-controlled government since the 1890s, and regional structures since 1939. Although the Queensland government maintained control until the 1980s, there has been an increase in Torres Strait Islander self-determination over time.

The Torres Strait Regional Authority

The Torres Strait Regional Authority (TSRA) is an Australian government statutory authority set up in 1994 to advise the federal Minister for Families, Housing, Community Services and Indigenous Affairs on matters relating to the Torres Strait, and it managed to escape the fate of ATSIC in 2005. The officials who work for the authority develop, organise and run programs aimed at helping Torres Strait Islanders manage our own affairs in everything from economic development and employment to native title, housing and environmental health. Their approach is based on the unique Ailan Kastom Bilong Torres Strait — Torres Strait Islander culture.

Corporations (Aboriginal and Torres Strait Islander) Act 2006 (Cth) (CATSI Act)

The *CATSI Act* came into force on 1 July 2007 for the incorporation and regulation of Aboriginal and Torres Strait Islander corporations. Whilst some CATSI corporations perform government style functions over vast areas and populations, Indigenous Australian peoples are presently compelled to incorporate to exercise these functions rather than be acknowledged as self-governing sovereign peoples. (Incorporation is the legal process used to form a corporate entity or company — a corporation is a separate legal entity from its owners, with its own rights and obligations.)

Today there are an estimated 2,781 local, regional and national Aboriginal and Torres Strait Islander incorporated organisations. There are also numerous unincorporated community-based working groups, alliances and committees. Although some community-controlled organisations are large and have strong national networks, many are managed by voluntary committees, have basic administrative systems and are heavily reliant on the work of a small number of key personnel. According to the Office of the Registrar of Indigenous Corporations, the top five hundred Indigenous corporations manage assets in excess of $2.2 billion and employ 11,095 people.

Making legal decisions for our communities

The recognition of our customary law within the criminal justice system is a complex and difficult issue, which has been criticised and, in a few cases, sensationalised in the popular media. As a result, there are many misconceptions in the wider Australian community. Customary law has not been taken into account by the courts when judging someone's guilt or innocence; rather it has been used primarily in sentencing people already convicted of crimes.

The non-Indigenous criminal justice system sometimes emphasises punishment over rehabilitation in the way it deals with criminal behaviour. Our community-based approaches try to bridge the gap between the expectations of both the victims and the perpetrators for the best possible outcome.

There are a number of Aboriginal Courts that have been established and other reforms that seek to include the involvement of our elders as part of the criminal justice system: such as the Koori Courts in Victoria and the Nunga Courts that have a role in the sentencing of Indigenous offenders in South Australia. Unfortunately, the only way our peoples can come before our elders and senior decision-makers is if they plead guilty to an offence. The finding of guilt or innocence is still determined by judicial officers, such as judges and magistrates.

One example of engaging elders in sentencing is the use of the Circle Sentencing program in NSW, where community elders and a facilitator, along with the person convicted of the offence, and sometimes those who were the victims of the offence, meet in a circle. The matter is discussed, and a joint decision is agreed about an appropriate sentence. Our elders provide no easy options, and some who work in the justice system believe that the sentences they hand out are tougher than those given in the society at large. However, our elders also work hard to keep young people out of the prison system and to promote healing and well-being. They factor in the intergenerational effects of trauma that stem from colonisation and the Stolen Generations and the continuing issues that stem from poverty for our peoples.

Every state as well as the Northern Territory now has an Aboriginal Legal Service.

Indigenous representatives of the Royal Australian Air Force and people of Wiradjuri country, cousins Leading Aircraftmen Brent Irvine (left) and Jackson Saddler, proudly display the Aboriginal flag in support of NAIDOC Week 2017 at the main air operating base in the Middle East Region. © Commonwealth of Australia, Department of Defence

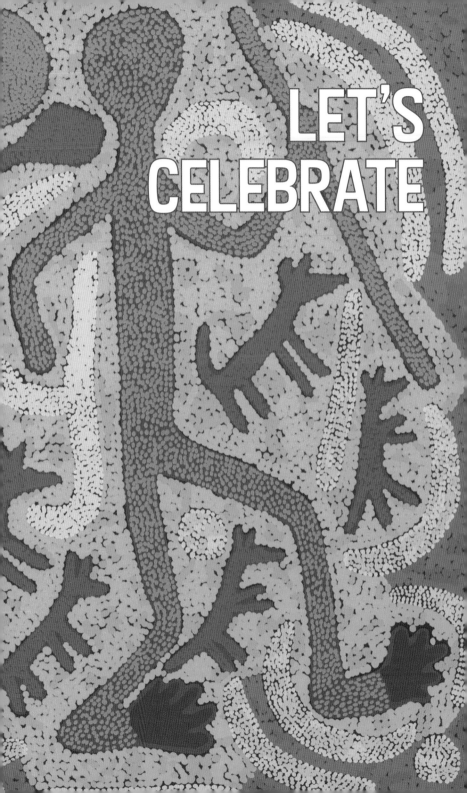

LET'S
CELEBRATE

RECONCILIATION

The reconciliation movement began with an effort by Australians to acknowledge the wrongs done to us, to promise that such actions would never be repeated, and to adopt measures to repair the pain and loss we have experienced. Reconciliation requires that Australia acknowledges the manner in which it acquired the land and the fact that it has frequently crushed our attempts to seek common justice. Some of us don't believe we need to be the ones taking the lead in reconciliation; others believe Indigenous and non-Indigenous Australians need to work together. Some non-Indigenous Australians oppose reconciliation or apologies for past practices, believing that they are not responsible for the actions of previous generations, or governments.

Sydney Harbour Bridge during the Walk for Reconciliation, Corroboree 2000, with the Aboriginal flag flying beside the Australian flag. Photo: Loui Seselja, National Library of Australia, nla.pic-an24526893

Bob Hawke, Prime Minister from 1983 to 1991, made a promise, following a second bark petition presented to the Commonwealth Parliament, that his government would work toward a treaty or compact. The government established the Council for Aboriginal Reconciliation (CAR) in 1991 and it operated for ten years to promote reconciliation and advise the government on formal ways by which reconciliation could be achieved.

Groups like Australians for Native Title and Reconciliation (AnTaR) and Reconciliation Australia work steadily for reconciliation, as did the former CAR, which was headed by Patrick Dodson and Evelyn Scott. Many Australians have participated in the Sea of Hands, a national public art installation initiated by AnTaR, where people sign a hand-shaped sign to reflect their commitment to justice for Indigenous Australian peoples, and it has travelled the country. In 2000, at the release of the final reports of CAR, many thousands of people walked across Melbourne's Princes Bridge and hundreds of thousands across Sydney's Harbour Bridge, while other states had similar massive gatherings, in a national expression of a desire for reconciliation.

National Reconciliation Week, an initiative of Reconciliation Australia, takes place every year in May and provides an opportunity for all Australians to learn about our histories, cultures and achievements. Organisations, schools and individuals are encouraged to organise events that celebrate and promote respectful relationships between non-Indigenous and Aboriginal and Torres Strait Islander peoples.

Plans for action

Reconciliation Action Plans (or RAPs) assist organisations to build relationships between Indigenous and non-Indigenous Australians. They allow everyone to make a public contribution to the national reconciliation effort. International experience and the growing evidence of what works reveal the essential ingredient: respectful partnerships between Indigenous and non-Indigenous Australians.

Melbourne Football Club RAP launch with (l–r) past Melbourne player Aaron Davey, co-captain Jack Viney, past player Austin Wonaeamirri, club Chairman Glen Bartlett, past player Liam Jurrah, co-captain Nathan Jones and past player Neville Jetta. Photo: Melbourne Football Club

NAIDOC WEEK

NAIDOC Week is about every Australian celebrating the First Australians, the oldest surviving cultures in the world. Celebrated around the country every July, it has its origins in the fight for Aboriginal rights that began in the 1920s and 1930s, when groups like the Australian Aboriginal Progressive Association and the Australian Aborigines' League drew attention to our poor living conditions and our lack of citizenship rights. In 1957, a National Aborigines Day Observance Committee was formed, supported by federal and state governments, the churches and major Aboriginal and Torres Strait Islander organisations. In 1988 the committee's name was changed to National Aborigines and Islanders Day Observance Committee (NAIDOC) to acknowledge Torres Strait Islander peoples as well. Over time, the name of the committee has evolved into the name for the whole week. We take great pride in NAIDOC Week and there are plenty of events going on around the country where all people are welcome and appreciated.

FESTIVALS AND TOURS

There are many celebrations of Aboriginal and Torres Strait Islander cultures throughout the year across Australia. The following includes just a few of them that you may want to take part in.

On 26 January each year, Sydney hosts the Yabun Festival of Arts and Aboriginal culture. Also in January, the popular Undalup Birak Festival in Western Australia celebrates Noongar culture. In April, people can see the Deadly Funny Competition as part of the comedy festival in Melbourne, or attend Nayri Niara Good Spirit Festival on Bruny Island, Tasmania. In June there's the Burunga Festival and in August there is Garma, a five-day festival of the Yolngu people's traditional culture in Arnhem Land. In September, every two years, Thursday Island hosts a Torres Strait Islander culture festival called Winds of Zenadth. Each October there is a four-day dance festival in Laura, Queensland called

Murray Island Dance Group members (l–r) Sarah Mabo, Suramina Tabo, Jezebel Gisu, Tanya Wailu and Lilimea Mabo perform at the opening of Cairns NAIDOC Week 2017 at Fogarty Park. Photo: Stewart McLean

The Welcome Ceremony at Tasmania's 2017 Nayri Niara Good Spirit Festival.
Photo: Nikki Michail

the Laura Dance and Cultural Festival, and a four-day cultural festival, Yarnballa, at Port Augusta, South Australia.

There are also special dates on the calendar put aside to mark the achievements of Indigenous artists and community leaders across Australia. The National Indigenous Arts Awards, which are held in May, celebrate music, dances, visual art and literature. NAIDOC Week in the first week of July celebrates the history, culture and achievements of Aboriginal and Torres Strait Islander peoples. Awards are given to people who have been outstanding in areas such as sport and the arts, or in the Indigenous Australian community in general. In August, the Telstra Aboriginal and Torres Strait Islander Art Awards give prizes for visual artists.

Most Aboriginal and Torres Strait Islander festivals fully encourage the participation of visitors. Check the internet and look for festivals in your area or the area you are visiting and prepare to be entertained and informed.

The Koorie Heritage Trust houses public exhibition spaces featuring important works from both established and emerging Koorie artists. Image supplied by the Koorie Heritage Trust. Photographer Peter Bennett, 2015.

The Koorie Heritage Trust, Melbourne, is an important Aboriginal cultural centre including the only public collection dedicated solely to Koorie art and culture, including an oral history collection and reference library. The Trust offers a range of public programs and services including an annual exhibition program, cultural workshops, an education service that includes guided walking tours, a Koorie Family History Service and a retail shop dedicated to showcasing the uniqueness of Victorian Aboriginal art and design.

Many Australian and overseas visitors are taking advantage of the increasing number of tourist programs operated by our communities. There is no better way to appreciate our cultures or the Australian environment than to hear it from us. Visitors can learn about mud-crabbing and trochus jewellery at the Ardyaloon Trochus Hatchery & Aquaculture Centre at One Arm Point (west Kimberley, Western Australia), or bush tucker and aquaculture at Lake Condah (Victoria), and contact with rare animals is the daily experience in the Desert Park at Alice Springs. There are rainforest tours at Queensland's Mossman Gorge, and guided walks on the Larapinta trail or the Adnyamathana lands of South Australia's Flinders Ranges. There are many groups offering first-class tourism experiences and you can usually find them through state and territory tourism organisations or online.

There are also many cultural centres throughout the country that welcome visitors. Tjapukai Aboriginal Cultural Park in Cairns in northern Queensland; Muru Mittigar Aboriginal and Cultural Education Centre in Castlereagh, New South Wales; Kooljaman at Cape Leveque in Western Australia's Kimberley; Bunjilaka Aboriginal Cultural Centre and the Koori Heritage Trust in Melbourne; and Gab Titui Cultural Centre on Thursday Island in the Torres Strait are just a few of the many cultural centres that exist.

KEEPING PLACES

Keeping places act as a vital part of maintaining and preserving culture within our communities, as well as providing places for learning for the wider community. They provide safe places for objects to be stored and allow us to determine how to tell their stories. They also allow us to promote our history and culture in our local areas, educate our young people about their history and traditional skills, and provide a meeting place for communities. When they are run as businesses there can be economic benefits through training and employment opportunities.

Many keeping places are also cultural centres that welcome visitors to share in our rich and diverse cultural heritage.

TRAVELLING RESPECTFULLY

Should you wish to visit our communities, you may find that there are organised tours, in many cases led by Indigenous Australians. If not, it is advisable to write, phone or fax the council in any community you wish to visit. There are some communities, especially in remote areas, where you need to seek permission to enter before your visit as it is legally privately held land. This also ensures your safety in remote and difficult terrain, and helps to protect the community from unwelcome intrusions, especially at times of mourning.

Some communities have areas of cultural and spiritual significance that are restricted to the general public, so it is always a good idea to ask whether or not such areas exist in the community you visit. For instance, it is inappropriate to swim in some waterholes and there are other areas that are restricted. Just as many cultures forbid the drinking of alcohol, there are many places in our country where it is not permitted.

As in any society, it is important to respect people's privacy and to dress appropriately. Remember, too, that for some Indigenous Australians English is a second or third language, and the people you speak to may not wish to divulge certain spiritual and cultural matters. Direct and forceful questions can be embarrassing to us. It is courteous to ask for permission before you take photos or video.

If you intend to take or publish photos — even if you just want to post them on your website or networking page — you should seek an individual's or community's permission before doing so. Explain how you might want to use the images, and, if commerce is involved, please consider sharing copyright. Obtain the names of the people in the photo or video so you can say who they are, and ask if people want copies of the photos sent to them. Although less common now, there are some communities whose members strenuously avoid seeing images of deceased relatives or hearing them in recordings for cultural and/or spiritual reasons. Seeing or hearing these things can be very distressing, so it is good to establish whether or not such prohibitions exist in the community you visit.

TIMELINE

This timeline is by no means exhaustive. It would be impossible to list in just a few pages all of the events that have influenced our lives in both positive and negative ways. The many massacres of our people cannot all be included, but that does not mean they did not happen. The events listed here are a just a representation of a few. Note that some of the pre-contact information is debated by academics and subject to revision as new knowledge becomes available.

BP = Before Present

At least 65,000 BP	Evidence of human occupation (stone axes and grindstones) on mainland Australia: much longer than modern humans have been in many parts of Europe and the Americas.
42,000 BP	A man from the Lake Mungo area is cremated and buried in a shallow grave, and liberally covered with powdered red ochre. This is one of the earliest known burials of distinctly modern people. The kind of cremation and the use of red ochre indicated sophisticated burial customs and the earliest known evidence of modern human spirituality.
28,000 BP	Aboriginal peoples paint images on the walls of caves throughout Arnhem Land depicting a number of now-extinct Australian animals.
20,000–15,000 BP	Deep in caves under the Nullarbor Plains at Koonalda, South Australia, Aboriginal peoples mine flint and leave grooved designs on the cave walls.
18,000 BP	Grindstones are used for hard fruits, seeds and vegetables and in ochre preparation in Arnhem Land.
13,000–12,000 BP	At the end of the glacial period the seas rise, separating Tasmania from the mainland.

13,000–9500 BP	Several people are buried in different positions in the Kow Swamp in northern Victoria, suggesting complex mortuary rituals.
9000 BP	Aboriginal peoples at Wyrie Swamp in south-east South Australia use returning boomerangs to catch waterfowl.
5000 BP	A new, small-tool technology is developing in south-eastern Australia. By 3000 BP the technology has spread as far as Cape York.
1451	Dutch documents record the journeys of Macassan trepangers (those seeking sea-cucumber) to 'Marege', as the Macassans called Australia. They introduce tobacco and canoes.
1606	Spanish mariner, Luis Vaez de Torres, becomes the first European to travel through what is now called the Torres Strait.
1623	Dutchman Willem van Colster's exploratory voyage is the first recorded European contact with Aboriginal peoples in Arnhem Land.
1770	Lieutenant James Cook claims possession of the whole east coast of Australia by raising the British flag at Possession Island in the Torres Strait, just off the northern tip of Cape York Peninsula.
1788	Captain Arthur Phillip raises the British Flag at Sydney Cove and white colonisation begins. The population of Aboriginal and Torres Strait Islander peoples is estimated to be more than 750,000 across the continent.
1789	Less than a year after the arrival of the First Fleet, an outbreak of a smallpox-like disease is thought to have led to the death of 50 to 90 per cent of the Aboriginal population of the Sydney Town area. Further epidemics of disease followed as did murders and massacres, dispossession of land and destruction of material culture.

1792	Young Eora man, Bennelong, along with Cadigal man Colebee are abducted and taken to Governor Phillip's house, Sydney, to act as mediators between the British and Aboriginal peoples.
1803	Van Diemen's Land (Tasmania) is invaded, and several violent clashes ensue.
1824	Conflict between non-Aboriginal and Aboriginal people in the Bathurst district of central western NSW becomes so serious that martial law is proclaimed from August to December.
1829	The British invade Western Australia. In 1834, Western Australia's Governor Stirling leads twenty-five mounted police against Aboriginal people following attacks on the white invaders. Official records show fourteen Aboriginal people are shot in what's now called the 'Battle of Pinjarra'; Aboriginal testimonies suggest that far more were killed.
1830	In what has become known as the 'Black War' Governor Arthur tries unsuccessfully to drive all the remaining Aboriginal people in eastern Van Diemen's Land on to the Tasman Peninsula. It is spectacularly unsuccessful in rounding up people but is a precursor to Aboriginal people later accepting George Augustus Robinson's suggestion to move to a Flinders Island settlement, before final repatriation to Tasmania in 1847.
1835	On the banks of the Merri Creek (today's Northcote suburb of Melbourne) John Batman claims to have signed a treaty with eight clan leaders of what he called the Dutigullar tribe for two tracts of land totalling approximately 600,000 acres. Batman offers blankets, knives, mirrors, tomahawks, scissors, clothing and flour in return. A few months later the New South Wales colonial government declares the treaty invalid, stating it was the British not the Kulin who would have sovereignty over land.

1837   The *Report from the Select Committee on Aborigines (British settlements)*, Great Britain House of Commons, concludes that local legislatures are 'unfit' to exercise jurisdiction over Aboriginal peoples and their lands. The colonisers ignore the report, and continue to claim Indigenous land as their own.

1838   The first Aboriginal Protectorate is established for Port Philip in Victoria.

At Myall Creek near Inverell in NSW, twenty-eight Aboriginal people are shot by twelve non-Aboriginal men. Seven of the murderers are hung in December and there is public outrage that European men should be convicted for the murder of Aboriginal Australians.

1848   NSW native police troopers are hired and brought to Queensland to track and kill wanted Aboriginal people with whom they have no kinship or alliance, and to help open up the land for settlement.

1851   The colony of Victoria is proclaimed.

1869   The *Aboriginal Protection Act 1869* is passed in Victoria, giving the Board for the Protection of Aborigines an extraordinary level of control over Aboriginal peoples' lives.

1871   The London Missionary Society, led by Rev. Samuel MacFarlane, lands on Erub (Darnley) Island in the Torres Strait.

1894   Bunuba man, Jandamarra, a skilled stockman, leads an armed insurgency in the Kimberley. An outlaw to some, a hero to others, his guerrilla war against police and pastoralists lasts for three years.

1906   The peoples of the Great Sandy Desert experience their first contact with white settlers when Canning's survey team travel 2,000 km from Wiluna in Western Australia, surveying the desert and in search of water. The route becomes known as the Canning Stock Route.

1918	The Aborigines Ordinance in the Northern Territory combines the 1910 Act (SA) and the 1911 Ordinance (Cth), giving the Chief Protector wide-ranging powers over Aboriginal peoples.
1926	Aboriginal people are murdered by police following the spearing of a pastoralist in what's now called the Forrest River Massacre. Two policemen are charged but the case was dropped due to lack of evidence. The 1927 Royal Commission to Inquire into Alleged Killing and Burning of Bodies of Aborigines in the East Kimberly is established. Subsequently, governments were pressured to improve the circumstances of Aboriginal peoples.
1927	The Western Australian government declares central Perth a prohibited area for Aboriginal people. They can only enter with a 'native pass', which is issued by the Commissioner of Native Affairs. This lasts until 1954.
1931	Arnhem Land in the Northern Territory is declared an Aboriginal reserve.
1942	Darwin is bombed by the Japanese and many Aboriginal people are relocated in 'control camps', with restrictions placed on their movement. In Arnhem Land, Aboriginal people are recruited into the Northern Territory Special Reconnaissance Unit to defend against the anticipated Japanese invasion.
1949	Aboriginal people who served in the Second World War gain the right to enrol to vote under the Commonwealth Electoral Act.
1953	The first of three British nuclear tests is conducted at Emu Field in South Australia, leaving many Aboriginal people suffering from radiation sickness.
1957	The Federal Council for the Advancement of Aborigines and Torres Strait Islanders (FCMTSI; later FCAATSI) is formed. It continues to petition for Indigenous rights for the next twenty-one years.

1962	The Commonwealth Electoral Act is amended to give Aboriginal people the right to enrol to vote in all states except Queensland.
1965	Aboriginal and Torres Strait Islander people in Queensland finally gain the right to enrol to vote in state elections.
1966	The Commonwealth government signs the International Convention on the Elimination of All Forms of Racial Discrimination.
	One-hundred-and-seventy Gurindji people walk off Lord Vestey's Wave Hill station in the Northern Territory. Originally understood as a strike against poor working conditions, the walk-off is primarily a demand for Gurindji autonomy and the return of traditional lands. The walk-off is a crucial moment in the step towards the *Aboriginal Land Rights (Northern Territory) Act 1976* (Cth).
1967	A referendum is held in May to change clauses in the Federal Constitution which discriminate against Aboriginal people. Nearly 91 per cent of Australians vote 'yes' for change, and as a result Indigenous people are included in the census and legislation concerning the welfare of Aboriginal people passes from state government to the Commonwealth government.
1971	Larrakia people 'sit-in' on Bagot Road, Darwin, in a protest against the theft of their land.
1972	The Aboriginal Heritage Act is declared in Western Australia.
	The Whitlam Government freezes all applications for mining and exploration on Commonwealth Aboriginal reserves.
	Establishing the Tent Embassy, four Aboriginal activists, Michael Anderson, Billy Craigie, Tony Coorey and Bertie Williams, erect a tent on the lawns of old Parliament House in Canberra, stating that they will stay until the government grants land rights.

1973	Mr Justice Woodward of the Aboriginal Land Commission delivers his first report, emphasising Aboriginal people's right to block mining on their land, and signalling a new approach to Aboriginal land rights.
1975	The World Council of Indigenous People is founded.
	The Aboriginal Land Fund Commission is established to buy land for Aboriginal groups across Australia.
	The Senate unanimously pass a resolution put by Senator Bonner which acknowledges prior Indigenous ownership of Australia, and provides compensation for dispossession of land.
	The *Racial Discrimination Act 1975* (Cth) is passed by the Whitlam Government. It overrides state and territory legislation and makes racial discrimination unlawful.
1976	Aboriginal law and land rights are finally recognised in the *Aboriginal Land Rights (Northern Territory) Act 1976* (Cth). Recognition of land ownership is extended to 11,000 Aboriginal people.
1978	The Northern Territory Aboriginal Sacred Sites Ordinance is passed, instituting prosecution for trespass and desecration of Aboriginal sites.
1980	International attention is drawn to Aboriginal land rights when Aboriginal people from around Australia travel to Western Australia's Noonkanbah to help the Yungnogora people fight to stop the Amax mining company from drilling on their land.
	The National Federation of Land Councils is formed, giving a national voice to the land rights movement.
1981	The *Pitjantjatjara Land Rights Act 1981* (SA) is passed and a large area of the state is returned to the Pitjantjatjara people.
1982	Aboriginal people at Ntaria (Hermannsburg mission), in central Australia are granted freehold title.

1984	The Western Australian Government introduces a land rights bill, but it is defeated in the upper house.
1987	Voting becomes compulsory for Aboriginal people in the Northern Territory elections.
1988	While many non-Indigenous Australians commemorate the bicentenary of the colonisation of the country, tens of thousands of Aboriginal and Torres Strait Islander people and some non-Indigenous Australians march through the streets of Sydney on 26 January to celebrate two hundred years of survival.

Prime Minister Hawke responds favourably to the suggestion of a treaty with Indigenous Australian peoples, but this is never realised. |
1989	The Aboriginal and Torres Strait Islander Commission (ATSIC) is established by the Federal Government.
1991	Legislation providing for land rights is passed through the Legislative Assembly in Queensland, but is markedly inferior to the standards set in the Northern Territory. Land rights legislation for Tasmanian Aboriginal peoples is rejected by the upper house.
1992	Prime Minister Paul Keating makes his 'Redfern Park' speech at the launch of the International Year of the World's Indigenous People, in which he acknowledges past wrongs.
1994	Minister for Aboriginal Affairs, Robert Tickner, places a 25-year ban on the construction of the Hindmarsh Island Bridge, after a group of Ngarrindjeri women claim that the island is sacred and the details cannot be publicly revealed. The 1995 Hindmarsh Island Royal Commission finds that claims of 'secret women's business' are a fabrication. The later 2001 Federal Court judgment finds that there was no fabrication of 'secret women's business'. The bridge is built, nonetheless.

2000 Athlete Cathy Freeman lights the cauldron at the 2000 Summer Olympics and goes on to win a gold medal in the 400-metres track event. Following her win, Freeman carries the Aboriginal and Australian flags in a victory lap around the stadium.

2007 The Commonwealth government announce a dramatic intervention into some Northern Territory Aboriginal communities in response to the *Little children are sacred* report. Against the recommendations of the report, the *Northern Territory National Emergency Response Act 2007* is passed, and sections of the *Racial Discrimination Act 1975* are repealed.

2008 Against the recommendations of the Northern Territory Emergency Response (NTER) review, the Australian government continues the Northern Territory Intervention for a further twelve months, with some changes.

The Prime Minister, Kevin Rudd, moves a motion in federal parliament to apologise to Australia's Indigenous peoples with specific reference to the Stolen Generations.

A High Court decision, known as the Blue Mud Bay decision, gives Traditional Owners native-title rights over the inter-tidal zone of Blue Mud Bay along the coastline of north-east Arnhem Land.

2009 Australia signs the *Declaration on the Rights of Indigenous Peoples* in 2009, after initially refusing along with Canada, the United States and New Zealand.

2010 The Queensland Parliament amends the state's constitution to include a preamble providing due recognition to Queensland's Aboriginal and Torres Strait Islander peoples.

Noongar man Ken Wyatt becomes the first Indigenous member of the House of Representatives in the federal parliament.

The first board of the National Congress of Australia's First Peoples, a representative body advocating for the recognition of Aboriginal and Torres Strait Islander peoples' rights, is appointed and the company becomes incorporated.

2012   The Aboriginal tent embassy celebrates its 40th anniversary.

The Panel on Constitutional Recognition of Indigenous Australians presents its report, *Recognising Aboriginal and Torres Strait Islander peoples in the constitution*, to Prime Minister Julia Gillard. In its report, the Panel unanimously endorses a specific proposal to amend the constitution.

Nova Peris becomes Senator for the Northern Territory and the first Aboriginal woman to enter federal parliament.

2015   Thousands of people rally in cities and towns around Australia to protest against the planned closure of around 150 remote Aboriginal communities in Western Australia.

The campaign against the forced closure of Aboriginal communities continues with a second international day of action, resulting in more than 85 rallies across Australia, New Zealand, Canada, Germany, Hawaii, Hong Kong, China, the UK and the USA.

2016   Aboriginal languages become a new HSC subject, seven years after the NSW Aboriginal Languages Policy was introduced.

The Kenbi land claim, Australia's longest running land claim, settles after thirty-seven years. The land claim stretches across the Cox Peninsula on the western side of Darwin Harbour and includes 65,000 hectares to be used by the Larrakia and the Belyuen people. The claim overcomes two extensive hearings, three Federal Court reviews and two High Court appeals.

Aboriginal leaders come together to announce the Redfern Statement, an urgent call for a more just approach to Aboriginal affairs and government action.

Linda Burney becomes the first female Aboriginal member of parliament in Australia's history after claiming the Federal seat of Barton. She is the first female Aboriginal member in the House of Representatives.

2016 (cont.)	The Federal Court finds police were racist during the 2004 riots on Palm Island. Justice Mortimer finds that police have contravened the Racial Discrimination Act in their treatment of Aboriginal witnesses, submitted inaccurate information to the coroner, and failed to 'communicate effectively' with the community to defuse tensions. They also state that Senior Sergeant Hurley should not have remained on the island or on duty.
2017	Ken Wyatt is appointed Minister for Aged Care and Indigenous Health, making him the first Aboriginal federal minister. It makes Mr Wyatt not only the first Aboriginal Australian elected to the House of Representatives and first to the frontbench, but also the first to lead a major portfolio.
	The co-Chairs of the National Congress of Australia's First Peoples and prominent Aboriginal leaders from across Australia formally present the Redfern Statement to parliamentary leaders in Canberra.
	More than 250 Aboriginal leaders from across the country gather at Uluru at the Referendum Council's National Convention to identify amendments required for constitutional recognition of Aboriginal people. The government rejects a proposal for a constitutionally enshrined voice to parliament.
	One of the longest-running native title cases (starting in 2003) comes to an end, with the Federal Court awarding exclusive rights over Pilbara land to the Yindjibarndi people. The land includes Fortescue Metals Group's Solomon Hub mine.
	The Uluru–Kata Tjuta National Park (UKTNP) board unanimously decides to close the Uluru climb on 26 October 2019.
2018	For the first time, Year 11 HSC students can learn about pre–1788 Aboriginal history in the same way they learn ancient Greek and Roman history, with a new Ancient Australia unit within the Ancient History Stage 6 syllabus.

MAPS

Australia

Torres Strait Islands including Cape York Peninsula

REFERENCES AND FURTHER READING

We see *The Little Red Yellow Black Book* as a stepping off point for readers to learn more themselves, or with others. The following references provide more detail about some of the subjects covered in this book. Because of the limits of space, the list is by no means exhaustive.

Australia has an abundance of excellent Aboriginal and Torres Strait Islander cultural creators and we recommend you explore their work.

Activism

Attwood, B 2003, *Rights for Aborigines*, Allen & Unwin, Crows Nest, NSW.

Attwood, B & Markus, A 2004, *Thinking black: William Cooper and the Australian Aborigines' League*, Aboriginal Studies Press, Canberra.

Broome, R 2001, *Aboriginal Australians: Black responses to white dominance 1788–2001*, 3rd edn, Allen & Unwin, St Leonards, NSW.

——2015, *Fighting hard: the Victorian Aborigines Advancement League*, Aboriginal Studies Press, Canberra.

Chesterman, J 2005, *Civil right: how Indigenous Australians won formal equality*, University of Queensland Press, St Lucia, Qld.

Goodall, H 2008, *Invasion to embassy: land in Aboriginal politics in New South Wales, 1770–1972*, Sydney University Press, Sydney.

Horner, J 2004, *Seeking racial justice: an insider's memoir of the movement for Aboriginal advancement, 1938–1978*, Aboriginal Studies Press, Canberra.

Kidd, R 2006, *Trustees on trial: recovering the stolen wages*, Aboriginal Studies Press, Canberra.

McGregor, R 1993, 'Protest and progress: Aboriginal activism in the 1930s', *Australian Historical Studies*, vol. 25, no. 101, pp. 555–68, DOI: 10.1080/10314619308595936.

——2009, 'Another nation: Aboriginal activism in the late 1960s and early 1970s, *Australian Historical Studies*, vol. 40, no. 3, pp. 343–60, DOI: 10.1080/10314610903105217.

REFERENCES

Maynard, J 2007, *Fight for liberty and freedom: the origins of Australian Aboriginal activism*, Aboriginal Studies Press, Canberra.

Taffe, S 2005, *Black and white together FCAATSI: the Federal Council for the Advancement of Aborigines and Torres Strait Islanders, 1958–1973*, University of Queensland Press, St Lucia, Qld.

Art

Birnberg, M & Krezmanski, J 2004, *Aboriginal artists dictionary of biographies: Western Deserts Central Desert and Kimberley region*, JB Publishing, Marleston, SA.

Eikelcamp, U 1999, *Don't ask for stories: women from Ernabella and their art*, Aboriginal Studies Press, Canberra.

Gibson, L 2013, *We don't do dots: Aboriginal art and culture in Wilcannia, New South Wales*, Sean Kingston Publishing, Herefordshire, UK.

Hinkson, M 2014, *Remembering the future: Warlpiri life through the prism of drawing*, Aboriginal Studies Press, Canberra.

Hutcherson, G 1998, *Gong-Wapitja: women and art from Yirrkala*, Aboriginal Studies Press, Canberra.

Janke, T & Quiggin, R 2007, *Protocols for producing Indigenous Australian Arts*, 2nd edn, (five booklets), Australia Council for the Arts, Strawberry Hills, NSW.

Kleinert, S & Neale, M (eds), 2000, *The Oxford companion to Aboriginal art and culture*, Oxford University Press, Melbourne.

McLean, I (ed.) 2011, *How Aborigines invented the idea of contemporary art*, Institute of Modern Art and Power Publications, Sydney.

Mosby, T 1998, *Ilan Pasin — This is our way: Torres Strait art*, The Gallery, Cairns, Qld.

Mowaljarlai, D & Malnic, J 2001, *Yorro Yorro Aboriginal Creation and the renewal of nature — rock paintings and stories from the Australian Kimberley*, 2nd edn, Magabala Books, Broome, WA.

Vivid Sydney, 'Songlines to illuminate the Sydney Opera House Sails for Vivid', media release, Sydney, 26 May 2016.

Volkenandt, C & Kaufmann, C 2009, *Between Indigenous Australia and Europe: John Mawurndjul*, Aboriginal Studies Press, Canberra.

Cultural studies

Collins, F & Davis, T 2004, *Australian cinema after Mabo*, Cambridge University Press, Melbourne.

Cowlishaw, G 2009, *The city's outback*, UNSW Press, Sydney.

Lydon, J 2014, *Calling the shots: Aboriginal photographies*, Aboriginal Studies Press, Canberra.

Moreton-Robinson, A 2004, *Whitening race: essays in social and cultural criticism*, Aboriginal Studies Press, Canberra.

Merlan, F 1998, *Caging the rainbow: places, politics, and Aborigines in a North Australian town*, University of Hawai'i Press, Honolulu.

Myers, F 1991, *Pintupi Country, Pintupi self: sentiment, place and politics among Western Desert Aborigines*, University of California Press, Berkeley, CA.

Nakata, M 2007, *Disciplining the savages: savaging the disciplines*, Aboriginal Studies Press, Canberra.

Read, P 1996, *Returning to nothing: the meaning of lost places*, Cambridge University Press, Cambridge.

Smith, L 2012, *Decolonising methodologies: research and Indigenous Peoples*, 2nd edn, Zed Books, London.

Education

Beresford, Q & Partington, G (eds) 2003, *Reform and resistance in Aboriginal education: the Australian experience*, University of Western Australia Press, Nedlands, WA.

Nicholls, C 2008, 'Death by a thousand cuts: Indigenous language bilingual education programmes in the Northern Territory of Australia, 1972–1998', *International Journal of Bilingual Education and Bilingualism*, vol. 8, no. 2–3, pp. 160–77, DOI: 10.1080/13670050508668604.

Employment

AIATSIS 2007, *Maps to success: successful strategies in Indigenous organisations*, AIATSIS, Canberra.

Environment and economic management

Gammage, B 2011, *The biggest estate on earth: how Aborigines made Australia*, Allen & Unwin, Sydney.

Pascoe, B 2014, *Dark emu*, Magabala Books, Broome, WA.

REFERENCES

Sen, A 1999, *Development as freedom*, Oxford University Press, New York.

Weir, J 2009, *Murray River Country: an ecological dialogue with Traditional Owners*, Aboriginal Studies Press, Canberra.

Weir, J, Stacey, C & Youngentob, K 2011, *The benefits of caring for country: a review of the literature*, report prepared for the Australian Government Department of Sustainability, Environment, Water, Population and Communities, AIATSIS, Canberra.

General reference

Arthur, W & Morphy, F (eds) 2005, *Macquarie atlas of Indigenous Australia: culture and society through space and time*, Macquarie Library, North Ryde, NSW.

Behrendt, L 2012, *Indigenous Australia for dummies*, Wiley Publishing, Milton, Qld.

Bird-Rose, D 2000, *Dingo makes us human*, Cambridge University Press, Melbourne.

Fletcher, E 2004, *Indigenous family history research: family history for beginners and beyond,* Heraldry & Genealogy Society of Canberra, Canberra, ACT.

Horton, D (ed.) 1994, *The encyclopaedia of Aboriginal Australia: Aboriginal and Torres Strait Islander history, society and culture*, Aboriginal Studies Press, Canberra.

Jenkins, M in Braithwaite, A 2016, 'Meet Misty Jenkins, who spends her days studying microscopic cancer killers', *SBS*, 18 May, <https://www.sbs.com.au/topics/science/fundamentals/article/2016/05/18/meet-misty-jenkins-who-spends-her-days-studying-microscopic-cancer-killers>.

Jupp, J (ed.) 2001, *The Australian people: an encyclopedia of the nation, its people and their origins*, 2nd edn, Cambridge University Press, Oakleigh, VIC.

Kleinert, S & Neale, M (eds) 2000, *The Oxford companion to Aboriginal art and culture*, Oxford University Press, Melbourne, VIC.

Macinnis, P 2013, *The big book of Australian history*, National Library of Australia, Canberra.

Mulvaney, D & White, J 1987, *Australians to 1788*, Syme & Weldon Associates, Broadway, NSW.

Olive, M in Macdonald, H 2016, 'Noma puts native food back on the menu', *ABC*, 27 January, <http://www.abc.net.au/radionational/programs/breakfast/noma-pop-up-puts-spotlight-on-native-foods/7118496>.

Reynolds, A 2006, *Keeping culture: Aboriginal Tasmania*, National Museum of Australia, Canberra.

Ryan, L 2012, *The Tasmanian Aborigines: a history since 1803*, Allen & Unwin, Sydney.

Smith, M 2013, *The archaeology of Australia's deserts*, Cambridge University Press, Cambridge.

Health

Carson, B (ed.) 2007, *Social determinants of Indigenous health*, Allen & Unwin, St Leonards, NSW.

Ganesharajah, C 2009, 'Indigenous health and wellbeing: the importance of Country', *Native Title Research Report*, no. 1, AIATSIS, Canberra.

Lee, T 2008, *Bureaucrats and bleeding hearts: Indigenous health in Northern Australia*, University of New South Wales Press, Sydney.

McCoy, B 2008, *Holding men: kanyirninpa and the health of Aboriginal men*, Aboriginal Studies Press, Canberra.

Silburn, K, Reich, H & Anderson, I (eds) 2016, *A global snapshot of Indigenous and tribal people's health: the Lancet-Lowitja Institute Collaboration*, The Lowitja Institute, Carlton, VIC.

Thorpe, A, Arabena, K, Sullivan, P, Silburn, K & Rowley, K 2016, *Engaging first peoples: a review of government engagement methods for developing health policy*, The Lowitja Institute, Carlton, VIC.

History

Broome, R 2005, *Aboriginal Victorians: a history since 1800*, Allen & Unwin, Sydney.

—— 2010, *Aboriginal Australians: a history since 1788*, Allen & Unwin, Sydney.

Clements, N 2014, 'Tasmania's black war: a tragic case of lest we remember?', *The Conversation*, 24 April, <https://theconversation.com/tasmanias-black-war-a-tragic-case-of-lest-we-remember-25663>.

Cole, A, Haskins, V & Paisley, F 2005, *Uncommon ground: white women in Aboriginal history*, Aboriginal Studies Press, Canberra.

Conor, L 2016, *Skin deep: settler impressions of Aboriginal women*, UWA Publishing, Perth.

Jebb, M 2003, *Blood, sweat and welfare: a history of white bosses and Aboriginal pastoral workers*, UWA Publishing, Perth.

—— & McGrath, A (eds) 2015, *Long history, deep time: deepening histories of place*, ANU Press, Canberra.

Pascoe, B 2007, *Convincing ground: learning to fall in love with your country*, Aboriginal Studies Press, Canberra.

Peterson, N & Myers, F (eds) 2016, *Experiments in self-determination: histories of the outstation movement in Australia*, ANU Press, Canberra.

Reynolds, H 2006, *The other side of the frontier: Aboriginal resistance to the European invasion of Australia*, UNSW Press, Sydney.

Sharp, N 1981, 'Culture clash in the Torres Strait Island: the maritime strike of 1936', *Journal of the Royal Historical Society of Queensland*, vol. 11:2, pp. 107–126.

Housing

Memmott, P 2007, *Gunyah, Goondie + Wurley: the Aboriginal architecture of Australia*, University of Queensland Press, St Lucia, Qld.

Identity

Carlson, B 2016, *The politics of identity: who counts as Aboriginal today?*, Aboriginal Studies Press, Canberra.

Fredericks, B 2013, 'We don't leave our identities at the city limits: Aboriginal and Torres Strait Islander people living in urban localities', *Australian Aboriginal Studies*, vol. 1, pp. 4–16.

Gorringe, S, Ross, J & Fforde, C 2011, '"Will the real Aborigine please stand up?" Strategies for breaking the stereotypes and changing the conversation', *AIATSIS Research Discussion Paper*, no. 28, AIATSIS, Canberra.

Grant, S 2015, 'The politics of identity: we are trapped in the imaginations of white Australians', *The Guardian*, 14 December, <http://www.theguardian.com/commentisfree/2015/dec/14/the-politics-of-identity-we-are-trapped-in-the-imaginations-of-white-australians>.

Grieves, V 2014, 'Culture, not colour, is the heart of Aboriginal Identity', *The Conversation*, 18 September, <https://theconversation.com/

culture-not-colour-is-the-heart-of-aboriginal-identity-30102>.

Turner, MK & Macdonald, B 2010, *Iwenhe Tyerrtye: what it means to be an Aboriginal person*, IAD Press, Alice Springs, NT.

Languages

Arthur, J 1996, *Aboriginal English: a cultural study*, Oxford University Press, Melbourne.

Clark, I & Heydon, T 2002, *Dictionary of Aboriginal placenames of Victoria*, Victorian Aboriginal Corporation for Languages, Melbourne.

Dobson, VP & Henderson, J 2013, *Anpernirrentye: kin and skin: talking about family in Arrernte*, IAD Press, Alice Springs, NT.

Eades, D 2013, *Aboriginal ways of using English*, Aboriginal Studies Press, Canberra.

Thieberger, T & McGregor, W (eds) 1994, *Macquarie Aboriginal words: a dictionary of words from Australian Aboriginal and Torres Strait Islander languages*, the Macquarie Library, Sydney.

Yallop, C & Walsh, M (eds) 2007, *Language and culture in Aboriginal Australia*, Aboriginal Studies Press, Canberra.

Law and land rights

Anaya, S 2004, *Indigenous peoples in International law*, 2nd edn, Oxford University Press, New York.

Bauman, T & Glick, L 2012, *The limits of change: Mabo and native title 20 years on*, AIATSIS, Canberra.

Bauman, T, Strelein, L & Weir, J (eds) 2013, *Living with native title: the experiences of Registered Native Title Corporations*, AIATSIS, Canberra.

Goot, M & Rowse, T 1994, *Make a better offer: the politics of Mabo*, Pluto Press, Leichhardt, NSW.

Janke, T 1997, *Our culture our future: report on Australian Indigenous cultural and intellectual property rights,* AIATSIS and ATSIC, Canberra.

Langton, M & Mazel, O 2008, 'Poverty in the midst of plenty: Aboriginal people, the "resource curse" and Australia's mining boom', *Journal of Energy and Natural Resources Law*, vol. 26, pp. 31–65,
DOI: 10.1080/02646811.2008.11435177.

REFERENCES

Langton, M, Mazel, O, Palmer, L, Shain, K & Tehan, M (eds) 2006, *Settling with Indigenous peoples: modern treaty and agreement making*, Federation Press, Sydney.

Norman, H 2015, *'What do we want?' A political history of Aboriginal land rights in New South Wales*, Aboriginal Studies Press, Canberra.

Read, P 2000, *Belonging: Australians, place and Aboriginal ownership*, Cambridge University Press, Cambridge.

Ritter, D 2009, *Contesting native title*, Allen & Unwin, Sydney.

Skyring, F 2011, *Justice: a history of the Aboriginal Legal Service of WA*, UWA Publishing, Perth.

Strelein, L 2009, *Compromised jurisprudence: native title cases since Mabo*, 2nd edn, Aboriginal Studies Press, Canberra.

Memoir

Beresford, Q 2006, *Rob Riley: an Aboriginal leader's quest for justice*, Aboriginal Studies Press, Canberra.

Booth, A & Briscoe, L 2015, '20 inspiring black women who have changed Australia', *NITV*, 6 March.

Central Land Council & Bowman, M (eds) 2015, *Every hill got a story*, Hardie Grant, Melbourne.

Charola, E & Meakins, F (eds) 2016, *Yijarni: true stories from Gurindji country*, Aboriginal Studies Press, Canberra.

Collard-Spratt, R & Ferro, J 2017, *Alice's daughter: lost mission child*, Aboriginal Studies Press, Canberra.

Dan, H & Neuenfeldt, K 2013, *Steady steady: the life and music of Seaman Dan*, Aboriginal Studies Press, Canberra.

Faulkner, S & Drummond, A 2007, *Life b'long Ali Drummond: a life in the Torres Strait*, Aboriginal Studies Press, Canberra.

Hale, M 2012, *Kurlumarniny: we come from the desert*, Aboriginal Studies Press, Canberra.

Harrison, K 1975, *Dark man, white world: a portrait of tenor Harold Blair*, Novalit Australia, Melbourne.

Kartinyeri, D & Anderson, S 2008, *Doreen Kartinyeri: my Ngarrindjeri calling*, Aboriginal Studies Press, Canberra.

Keeffe, K 2003, *Paddy's road: life stories of Patrick Dodson*, Aboriginal Studies Press, Canberra.

Kinnane, S 2003, *Shadow lines*, Fremantle Press, WA.

Kruger, A & Waterford, G 2007, *Alone on the soaks: the life and times of Alex Kruger*, IAD Press, Alice Springs, NT.

Lawford, E et al. & Marshall, P (ed.) 1989, *Raparapa kularr martuwarra: all right, now we go 'side the river, along that sundown way: stories from the Fitzroy River drovers,* Magabala Books, Broome, WA.

Mahood, K 2010, 'Songlines and faultlines', *Griffith Review*, no. 28, 14 December, pp. 53–5.

Martin, J & Shaw B 2011, *Joan Martin (Yaarna): a Widi woman*, Aboriginal Studies Press, Canberra.

Morgan, S 1988, *My place*, Fremantle Press, Fremantle, WA.

Neidjie, B & Lang, M 2015, *Old man's story: the last thoughts of Kakadu Elder Bill Neidjie*, Aboriginal Studies Press, Canberra.

Paisley, F 2012, *The lone protestor: AM Fernando in Australia and Europe*, Aboriginal Studies Press, Canberra.

Read, J & Coppin, P 2014, *Kangkushot: the life of Nyamal lawman Peter Coppin*, Aboriginal Studies Press, Canberra.

Rubuntja, W & Green, J 2002, *The town grew up dancing: the life and art of Wenten Rubuntja*, Jukurrpa Books, Perth.

Simon, B, Montgomerie, J & Tuscano, J 2009, *Back on the block: Bill Simon's story*, Aboriginal Studies Press, Canberra.

St Leon, M 1994, *The wizard of the wire: the story of Con Colleano*, Aboriginal Studies Press, Canberra.

Taylor, G 1999, *Albert Namatjira*, Cambridge University Press, Melbourne.

Military service

Beaumont, J & Cadzow, A 2018, *Serving our country: Indigenous Australians, war, defence and citizenship*, New South Publishing, Sydney.

Hall, R 1995, *Fighters from the fringe: Aborigines and Torres Strait Islanders recall the Second World War*, Aboriginal Studies Press, Canberra.

——1997, *The Black Diggers: Aborigines and Torres Strait Islanders in the Second World War*, Aboriginal Studies Press, Canberra.

REFERENCES

Jackomos, A & Fowler, D 1993, *Forgotten heroes: Aborigines at war from the Somme to Vietnam*, Victoria Press, South Melbourne.

Riseman, N & Trembath, R 2016, *Defending country: Aboriginal and Torres Strait Islander military service since 1945*, University of Queensland Press, St Lucia, Qld.

Music

Dunbar-Hall, P & Gibson, C 2004, *Deadly sounds, deadly places: contemporary Aboriginal music in Australia*, UNSW Press, Sydney.

Magowan, F & Neuenfeldt K (eds) 2005, *Landscapes of Indigenous performance: song and dance of the Torres Strait and Arnhem Land*, Aboriginal Studies Press, Canberra.

Haebich, A & Morrison J 2014, 'From karaoke to Noongaroke: a healing combination of past and present', in *Cultural Solutions (Griffith Review 44)*, TEXT Publishing, Sydney.

Policy and legislation

Attwood, B & Markus, A 2007, *The 1967 Referendum: race, power and the Australian Constitution*, Aboriginal Studies Press, Canberra.

Council for Aboriginal Reconciliation 2000, Roadmap for reconciliation, Council for Aboriginal Reconciliation, Canberra, <http://www.austlii.edu.au/au/other/IndigLRes/car/2000/10/>.

Davis, M & Williams, G 2015, *Everything you need to know about the referendum to recognise Indigenous Australians,* NewSouth Books, Sydney.

Davis, M & Langton, M (eds) 2016, *It's our country: Indigenous arguments for meaningful constitutional recognition and reform,* Melbourne University Press, Melbourne.

Moran, M 2016, *Serious whitefella stuff: when solutions became the problem in Indigenous affairs,* Melbourne University Press, Melbourne.

Rowse, T 2002, *Indigenous futures: choice and development for Aboriginal and Islander Australia*, UNSW Press, Sydney.

——2002, *White flour, white power: from rations to citizenship in Central Australia*, Cambridge University Press, Melbourne.

Wunan Foundation Inc. 2015, *Empowered communities: empowered peoples: design report*, Wunan Foundation, Sydney.

The Stolen Generations

Haebich, A 2000, *Broken Circles: Fragmenting Indigenous families 1800–2000*, Fremantle Arts Centre Press, Fremantle, WA.

Human Rights and Equal Opportunity Commission (HREOC) 1997, *Bringing them home: report of the National Inquiry into the Separation of Aboriginal and Torres Strait Islander Children from Their Families*, Australian Human Rights Commission, Sydney, <https://www.human-rights.gov.au/publications/bringing-them-home-report-1997>.

Sports

Gorman, S 2011, *Legends: the AFL Indigenous team of the century*, Aboriginal Studies Press, Canberra.

Maynard, J 2013, *Aborigines and the 'sport of kings': Aboriginal jockeys in Australian racing history*, Aboriginal Studies Press, Canberra.

Tatz, C & Tatz, P 2000, *Black Gold: the Aboriginal and Islander Sports Hall of Fame*, Aboriginal Studies Press, Canberra, ACT.

Tatz, C & Tatz, P 2018, *Black Pearls: the Aboriginal and Islander Sports Hall of Fame*, Aboriginal Studies Press, Canberra, ACT.

Torres Strait Islander history

Beckett, J 1990, *Torres Strait Islanders: custom and colonialism*, Cambridge University Press, Cambridge.

Davis, R (ed.) 2003, *Woven histories, dancing lives: Torres Strait Islander identity, culture and history*, Aboriginal Studies Press, Canberra.

Sharp, N 1993, *Stars of Tagai: the Torres Strait Islanders*, Aboriginal Studies Press, Canberra.

Travel and social history

Bauman, T 2006, *Aboriginal Darwin: a guide to exploring important sites of the past and present*, Aboriginal Studies Press, Canberra.

Eidelson, M 2014, *Melbourne Dreaming: a guide to important places of the past and present*, 2nd edn, Aboriginal Studies Press, Canberra.

REFERENCES

Hinkson, M & Harris, A 2010, *Aboriginal Sydney: a guide to important places of the past and present*, 2nd edn, Aboriginal Studies Press, Canberra.

Watson, D 2014, *The bush*, Penguin Group, Melbourne.

Writing and literature

Birch, T 2011, *Blood*, University of Queensland Press, St Lucia, Qld.

Heiss, A 2003, *Dhuuluu-Yala: to talk straight*, Aboriginal Studies Press, Canberra.

Heiss, A & Minter, (eds) P 2008, *Macquarie PEN anthology of Aboriginal literature*, Allen & Unwin, Crows Nest, NSW.

Lucashenko, M 2013, *Mullumbimby*, University of Queensland Press, St Lucia, Qld.

Pascoe, B 2016, *Dark Emu*, Magabala Books, Broome, WA.

Scott, K 1999, *Benang*, Fremantle Arts Centre Press, South Fremantle, WA.

——2009, *True Country*, Fremantle Press, Fremantle, WA.

Thomas, J 2016, *Songs that sound like blood*, Magabala Books, Broome, WA.

Van Toorn, P 2006, *Writing never arrives naked: early Aboriginal cultures of writing in Australia*, Aboriginal Studies Press, Canberra.

Wright, A 2006, *Carpentaria*, Giramondo Publishing, Artarmon, NSW.

——2013, *The swan book*, Giramondo Publishing, Artarmon, NSW.

Poetry

Cobby Eckermann, A 2012, *Ruby Moonlight: a novel of the impact of colonisation in mid-north South Australia around 1880*, Magabala Books, Broome, WA.

Davis, J 1988, *John Pat and other poems*, Dent, Melbourne.

Van Neerven, E 2016, *Comfort Foods*, University of Queensland Press, St Lucia, Qld.

Walker, K (Oodgeroo Noonuccal) 1964, *We are going*, Jacaranda Press, Brisbane.

Watson, SW 2001, *Hotel Bone*, Vagabond Press, Newtown, NSW.

ACKNOWLEDGMENTS

AIATSIS would like to acknowledge the assistance of Lawrence Bamblett and the following reviewers and contributors: Jude Barlow, Toni Bauman, Rhonda Collard-Spratt, Kayannie Denigan, Bhiamie Eckford-Williamson, Lizzie Ellis, Jacki Ferro, Hamish Gondarra and Rakuwan Gondarra, Stephen Hagan, Cedric Hassing, Mary Anne Jebb, Amanda Lissarangue, Doug Marmion, Miyarrka Media, Joy Murphy Wandin, Bill Simon, Jane Simpson, Luke Smyth, Robert Williams and Inge Kral.

INDEX

Note: a page number in italics indicates an image on that page.